SECOND CHOICE

Also by Viv Thomas
Future Leader

SECOND CHOICE

Embracing life as it is

VIV THOMAS

PATERNOSTER
PRESS

Copyright © 2000 Viv Thomas

First published 2000 by Paternoster Press.
Reprinted 2001, 2003

09 08 07 06 05 04 03   10 9 8 7 6 5 4

Paternoster Press is an imprint of Authentic Media,
PO Box 300, Carlisle, Cumbria CA3 0QS, UK
and Box 1047, Waynesboro, GA 30830-2047, USA

www.paternoster-publishing.com

British Library Cataloguing-in-Publication Data
A catalogue record for this book is available from the British Library

ISBN 1–84227–010–9

Cover design by Mainstream, Lancaster
Typeset by Waverley Typesetters, Galashiels
Printed and bound in Great Britain by
Cox & Wyman Ltd, Reading, Berkshire

For Rob and Brenda

Acknowledgements

There are many people who have helped to put this book together. Kate White, Kathi Tarantal and Jenny Pollock were all very helpful in the early stages. This was the period when I had no idea if this was a valuable project or not. Marie Morris has been her normal brilliant self throughout helping in many ways. Mark Finnie and all the people at Paternoster have done an excellent job in making this text see the light of day. Special thanks have to go to Alfy Franks, Dr R. Vishwanath, Rosemary Morris and all at O.M. India. Without their skill, experience and support this book would never ever have been written. I would not — and probably could not — have written this book without the love and support of Sheila Thomas

I am grateful to the following for permission to use copyright material:

Darton, Longman & Todd (Henri Nouwen — *Bread for the Journey*; Kenneth Leech — *Soul Friend*)

Wm B. Eerdmans (Eugene Peterson — *Working the Angles*)

Faber & Faber (Flannery O'Connor — *Wise Blood*)

HarperCollins London (C. S. Lewis — *Letters to Malcolm*)

HarperCollins New York (F. Buechner — *The Storm*)

Hutchinson (Brian Keenan — *An Evil Cradling*; Charles Handy — *The Empty Raincoat*)

Ignatius Press (Hans Urs von Balthasar — *Prayer*)

Inter-Varsity Press (Joyce Baldwin — *Daniel*; Chris Wright — *Living as the People of God*)

Leaftree (Susan Howatch — *Second Choice* © Leaftree Ltd 1995 reprinted with kind permission of the author)

Orbis (Henri Nouwen — *With Burning Hearts*)

Paternoster (Dewi Hughes — *God of the Poor*)

SPCK/CLC, USA (Amy Carmichael — *If*)

Walker Books (*Guess How Much I love You* — Text © 1994 Sam McBratney, illustrated by Anita Jeram. Reproduced by permission of the publisher, Walker Books, London)

Word (John Goldingay — *Daniel*)

Carver Yu (Carver Yu — *Being and Relation*)

Contents

Foreword

Most of us want to live as well as possible — get the most out of life, do our best, make a mark, work well, love and be loved, enjoy and give joy, and, finally, come to a good death. Given the near universality of what we intend, it is somewhat surprising that the human race doesn't get better as the centuries unfold. What we know and what we have has increased enormously but our bigger barns of information and technology and possessions don't seem to have done much for our souls. We aren't any better.

Some of us, when we realize this, start looking around for help. It doesn't take long to discover that there have always been a few men and women around who get noticed as 'wise' — the ones who live well and are able to guide others into living well. We call them in, adopting them as fathers and mothers, as friends and companions, as mentors and guides, to help us to live well, to live sane and whole, to live what our ancestors have been bold to name 'a holy life'. But it's easy to miss them. Their characteristically quiet voices don't call attention to themselves. Meanwhile the world is noisy with in-your-face self-promoting experts who get our attention by promising all sorts of excitement, power, longevity, health, serenity, prosperity and glamour. It doesn't take long to realize that none of them knows much about living well, what our Bibles name as eternal life, Real Life.

Wise men and women are there for the finding, but they don't give media interviews.

Viv Thomas in *Second Choice* has done his best to make sure that we don't miss one of the enduringly best of the 'wise,' namely, Daniel. Daniel, throughout our Jewish and Christian ancestry, has had an enormous influence in providing example and direction to people of faith for living at our best, living sane and faithful and holy. And especially during times when a faithful, sane and holy life seems totally irrelevant to what is held up by the culture as 'in'.

We are glutted with information but we are starved for wisdom. We know so much about everything under the sun, but we live astonishingly trivial lives. Why? Why do we know so much and live so badly? Well, partly at least because we as a culture are admiring all the wrong people and have lost touch with 'the wise'.

The wise person doesn't know more, he or she lives more. All the truth is lived truth for the wise, truth tested and refined and tempered in the crucible of street and market, bedroom and kitchen, cancer and rejection, children and marriage. Wisdom is lived truth.

I've never understood why Daniel, who for so long held a prominent position in the biblical pantheon of 'the wise', in our times became marginalized into a children's song ('Dare to be a Daniel') and depersonalized into a puzzle piece in a scenario for the End Time. But here he is, back again, with Viv Thomas's help, vigorous and robust as ever, living a holy life in an unholy time, a serious worshipper of God in a trivializing culture. His unholy time and trivializing culture are strikingly similar to our own. He continues as one of the best of the 'wise' whom God has given to those of us who follow Jesus, a wise companion in living sane and holy lives.

EUGENE H. PETERSON
Professor Emeritus of Spiritual Theology
Regent College, Vancouver B.C., Canada

Chapter One

Greeting second choice

I was on a preaching tour in Winnipeg, Canada in 1985. My wife was with me and we were trying to decide if I should take up a job which had been offered by a Christian charity in Toronto. We were in the middle of working and decision-making.

One of my decisions, a rash one as it turned out, was to go and have a game of golf on a public course. I hired some clubs but was told that the course was busy; would it be possible for me to join in a foursome with three people I did not know? After the introductions, when we exchanged names and occupations, my new golfing partners decided to call me 'Rev'.

My problem was that I don't play golf that well and I can go through years without visiting a course or striking a ball. This lack of practice can mean disaster when you do attempt to play, especially if you re-engage with the game in public, on a full course and playing with strangers. I started to feel uncomfortable and a little light-headed all at the same time, the sort of feeling you feel when you say yes but something inside says you should be saying 'no'. If I was to attempt to bungee jump today I think I could recreate the feelings of those moments.

So I found myself in a place which was not home, with a set of brand new relationships which I did not choose and about to demonstrate a skill which I did not have. What had looked like a good idea at one point in the afternoon was beginning to look like a bad idea only twenty minutes later. I was heading for golfing disaster.

The first six holes went very well and everything looked good with my golf game. The story began to unfold at the seventh hole. I was first to play and sliced the ball into some trees. This was not a great problem, as there were only seven or eight of them and there was considerable space in between each one. I saw the ball land safely. I wandered off to the trees and put my bag down but could not find my ball. I looked all over the area and after a while my playing companions came to help me. They saw it land, I saw it land, so where was it? Before long people from a parallel fairway came to search as well — even they had seen the ball land. But it was nowhere to be seen. With mounting frustration I had to admit the ball was lost and that I should lose a shot and take a fresh ball from my bag. I went to my bag, lifted it up — and underneath it lay my ball.

In one swoop of my golf bag I had made the day of my golfing partners. It was all very embarrassing and my companions enjoyed it a lot. One of them said, 'Hey Rev, you are really unusual!' The rest of the game was played without memorable incident. Perhaps the story is still being told in the clubs and restaurants of Winnipeg. I am sure I made an impression.

What was true of my golf game is frequently true about our lives. Often all we get is a 'second choice'. We are likely to find ourselves in lonely cities . . . doing soulless jobs . . . living with painful family relationships which looked promising at first but have now become damaging or even dangerous. We often have to live in places which are not home, with relationships which we do not really want, but we are expected to do it all with skill, wit and wisdom. Our reality is that we are not adequate for the task, we do not possess the resources to do all this well. This book is about that dilemma.

Choice, second choice and no choice

What we would like is to survey our options, look at the alternatives and then make our choice. This simple process radically shapes Western culture. To a significant extent we earn money, gain position and get educated in order to achieve a position in which we shall be able to respond to a range of choices. Money, position and education are intended to give us the power to go for our preferred options and make our choices. In our ideal world we choose our job, spouse, city, entertainment, company, community and religion at leisure with freedom. Most of us like to have our first choice.

In the real world things do not work that smoothly. Even if we have the opportunity to employ our power of choice, the first choice tends to go wrong. Somehow our first choice gets contaminated or corrupted; it changes and in the process we are changed along with it. What looked like an outstanding selection at first, turns into something less than we anticipated or much different. The attractive partner you married loses their appeal; the job with huge potential becomes tedious within a few weeks; the house where you felt so safe is burgled; and the friends to whom you once felt close are now distant. This is reality for many people and often we do not handle it well.

It did not take me long to realize that my own family was not the sort of family which would be other people's first choice. During my adolescent years it was not mine either. My father was dead, my mother was drinking heavily and our house was not the wonderful houses of some of my friends. We had little money and knew our place on the social ladder.

School was hard work, not because of the academic demands but because of my mother. My school was three minutes' walk away from home and this meant a permanent interaction with shame. At lunchtime the boys in my school would walk around town visiting shops and just hanging around street corners and they would do the same after school was over. Since my mother started drinking early in the day she would occasionally come home drunk, meeting my school friends as she did so.

The result for me was shame. For long periods of my adolescence I did not want her as my mother, did not want to live in that house, did not want to encounter the shame of what we were in town and especially at school. Regardless of my desires, my brother and I had to live there with all the trauma, turbulence and shame of what we were, but there were many times I would have loved to escape that world.

Yet there was another very positive side to this life I was living. God had made my brother and me tall, good at sport, able to hold our own academically and blessed us with the ability to laugh at ourselves. These were powerful counterweights to the other pressures. In a very profound way my mother believed in us. Often through the alcoholic haze of bad breath, beer-induced leglessness, torn tights, continual whining, explosions of temper and occasional filth, her love would come through. All of this was easier to handle for me, I was four years younger than my brother and he had to endure more than I did. We often had great times of joy with evenings of comfort and stability; the problem was that the next evening could be exactly the opposite. Now, thirty-five years later, I look back on all of the joy and the shame with a sense of mystery and wonder. I now own all the shame of those days and embrace it as part of the history of God's grace in my life. The shame has been transformed into grace; rather it has been consumed by grace. The water has been turned into wine. I now look back on those days with a sort of joy and laughter. Occasionally I do have a stab of pain but it is not to do with my brother, my mother, our home or shame, it is to do with others' responses to us: the feeling of being abandoned by people who could have helped. Yet my ability to look back at the events of my childhood with an open and positive heart did not help me at the time. For much of my early life I had to live in a context of second choice and no choice at all.

Learning from Daniel

The Scripture teaches that in the middle of these problems help is available. When you have to embrace life as it is there is no story more able to help than Daniel. (There is help from Jesus but that comes later in this book.)

Daniel, who is best known for the time he spent in the lions' den, began his life as a young man with an appalling 'second choice'. When the Babylonian army took Jerusalem Daniel was deported by the enemy. The Babylonians carted him off to Babylon. This was precisely the place where he did not want to be; he wanted to live in Jerusalem. The people he did not want to relate to were all the people who lived in Babylon. The culture of Babylon, its gods, food and language — all alien to him. The job eventually assigned to him was one he did not want — handling Babylon's administration. He had to respond continually to the dreams, whims, foolishness and political plotting of all the Kings he served. This was Daniel's life and Babylon was not even his second choice: in living there he had no choice at all.

Our Western culture calls us today to 'fulfil our potential'. The idea is that we have to live every moment to the maximum, squeezing the orange till we have drunk every drop. Worlds of second choice do not fit into this way of thinking. We often perceive second-choice worlds as inferior because many of them offer little glamour or 'self-actualization'. If only this or that could be put right we believe that we would then be able to live successfully and well. Second-choice worlds are somehow seen as the home of second-best people: people who do not know what they are doing. Second-choice worlds are inhabited by losers. The Daniel story confronts this sort of perfectionist thinking, shattering idealized fantasy worlds. Daniel insists that second-choice worlds are not dumping grounds for failures; they are rather arenas in which to demonstrate the reality of God. We may have been failures at school but our lack of education need not stop us learning how to do what God wants us to do here and now. We may be struggling to discover the reason why we have been born because so much of our lives has been deformed. Daniel teaches us that being deformed can explain to us what our lives are intended to be about. Daniel knew he was not complete and whole yet his life was focused and effective. In the latter chapters of the book we see Daniel is confused and unable to understand what God was saying but he was still given vision and power so he could do what God wanted him to do. Daniel also teaches us that it is possible to bring light into the darkness that surrounds us. Wicked people can be transformed, dark places can become places of brilliant light. Daniel teaches us that places of second choice can be first-class if we allow God to work them out.

Our second-choice worlds themselves remind us that the world in which we live is itself second choice and — to be honest — a mess. Yet, the mess and disappointment that surrounds us is often preferable to the deceptively smooth fantasy of living in our first-choice world. The whole world is disjointed and broken; it is not healed or mended, at least not yet. God has responded to our mess through careful planning and a series of huge initiatives. Things are not as they should be; the world is shattered and dislocated. We live our lives in the context of this dislocation, and we have to cope with our own second-choice worlds in a uniformly 'second-choice' context. Daniel had to live his life in two dislocations: living in a world already shattered by sin and rebellion, and embracing the people, the city, and culture of Babylon. We can learn from him if we want to deal with our own double dislocation.

Chapter Two

First-choice fantasy

> O Lord I cannot plead my love of thee:
> I plead thy love of me;
> The shallow conduit hails the unfathomable sea.
> (Christina Rossetti: *I cannot plead*)

> 'I love mankind,' he said, 'but I marvel at myself:
> the more I love mankind in general, the less I love
> human beings in particular.'
> (Fyodor Dostoyevsky: *The Brothers Karamazov*)

Before we can grasp the dimensions of our second-choice worlds we shall need to deal with a variety of aspirations, dreams and fantasies. These are the ideas we have about how our lives are supposed to be lived; they are the mental images which fill our minds as we walk down the street or put the shopping into the car.

In my idealized world I am a sporting hero. I score the goal that wins the Soccer World Cup for England; I breast the tape to win the 1500 metres at the Olympics. I have a golfing fantasy. As I walk home from the town centre I pass a certain flower shop — and occasionally the fantasy takes over. I imagine that I am playing a round of golf at Royal Birkdale, a course very near to where I used to play as a child. In my fantasy I am walking down the fairway and playing brilliantly. I win the British Open title and tell the interviewer that I am giving all the money I have won to charity. This is deep fantasy. I cannot play golf and if I could and did win I would not give all the money to charity, but when I walk past that flower shop the dream begins. I quite enjoy imagining the possibilities of this fantasy but I know it is only a dream. It will never happen.

Similar fantasies hold us when we think about our first-choice worlds. While they remain daydreams they are safe; when they become world-views they can destroy. Most of us live with fantasies. If only I had Tiger Woods's golfing skills ... Bill Gates's money ... Kate Moss's or Richard Gere's looks ... had won the lottery ... married him or her or gained a Ph.D. If we identify our fantasies and acknowledge that this is what they are, we will be able to face them and live more authentic lives.

Fantasy One: 'If I walk closely with God he will give me my first choice.'

The idea behind this fantasy is simple; it is the notion that spiritual people always 'get it right'. They listen to God and God always delivers to them the things they think they need. Really spiritual people are like high-class machinery — low maintenance and almost problem-free. If they do have problems they know how to solve them quickly.

Fantasy Two: 'In my first-choice world I will be happy.'

In this fantasy my peace and joy are dependent on getting my first choice. If I get what I want I will be truly happy and content. Anything which appears to me to be second best will not do, for it will not give me the joy I think I need, and thus make it impossible for me to live my life as I think I should be able to live it.

Fantasy Three: 'In my first-choice world I will be secure.'

If I get what I want I will be able to build my life with minimal risk. The underlying idea is that I do really know what is best for me so that I can actually make sure that I live a life which is long, safe and satisfied and under my control. In this fantasy, second-choice worlds are perceived as risky, difficult, undesirable and unstable.

Fantasy Four: 'In my first-choice world I will be able to walk close to God.'

This fantasy promises that when I am where I want to be then I can have a wonderful relationship with God. When I get my first-choice world it will help me understand his beauty, wonder and glory. In effect, as soon as I achieve this or that relationship, house, degree or piece of technology — then God and I will really be able to get on well together and I will be able to do more for him. Reality is different. It is possible to walk closely with God while our lives are looking like a disaster zone; to get precisely what we want and feel thoroughly miserable; to make decisions which are intended to make us feel safe yet be dominated by fear; to achieve near perfection in our lives but feel that God is no more than a distant idea.

Fortunately, we have stories like Daniel's so we can be re-orientated, led out of abstraction and fantasy, and introduced to life as it is intended to be lived.

PART ONE

Encountering your second-choice world

Chapter Three

Initiation

Somehow, in the midst of our tears, a gift is
hidden. Somehow, in the midst of our mourning,
the first steps of the dance take place. Somehow,
the cries that well up from our losses belong to
our song of gratitude.
(Henri J. M. Nouwen: *With Burning Hearts*[1])

*And the Lord delivered Jehoiakim king of Judah
into his hand, along with some of the articles
from the temple of God.* (Daniel 1:2)

Like many people who have to live in worlds of second
choice Daniel had many reasons to complain. His life took
a turn which was not of his choosing. A rampaging King
Nebuchadnezzar brought him, along with many of the
best of the Hebrews, to Babylon. The exile which followed,
like many experiences of second choice, had a clear cause.
Yet — and surprisingly — these events did not begin with
Nebuchadnezzar's aggression. The roots of this Babylonian
second-choice world began with the Hebrews themselves
and their own relationship with God. The Hebrews entered

---

[1] p. 28.

into a world of second choice because of their inability to listen to what God was saying.

Not all second-choice worlds begin with disobedience to God, but Daniel and the Hebrews were carried off to Babylon in 605 BC because 'they mocked God's messengers, despised his words, and scoffed at his prophets until the wrath of God was aroused and there was no remedy'.[2] In short they had messed up their relationship with God with profound but very human stupidity. Daniel found himself in a place he did not want to be and the primary cause of his difficulty was the wrongdoing of other people, many of whom were now dead.

Sometimes our second-choice worlds result from the failures, initiatives, stupidities and decision-making of others and we just have to cope with the results of both the restrictions consequently imposed on us and the opportunities offered. Daniel had to operate in these sorts of conditions. He was doubly a victim: not only was he taken into exile but it was the fault of others that he was there. What is remarkable about his life is how he dealt with these realities; he coped with being a victim, and from being a hapless captive became a major influence over a hostile nation.

It is important to remember that Daniel lived the whole of his life in a world which was controlled by Babylonian kings, politicians and officials. Never in control of his own destiny, he was always someone's servant and had to be shaped constantly by the agenda of others. His life was one long adjustment to other peoples' thoughts, fears, passions and addictions.

At first glance Daniel appears doomed to be a failure. He does not fit our modern image of success. Our culture

---

[2] 2 Chronicles 36:15–21.

tells us that successful people build their own worlds by making choices that they can control along with their consequences. People who cannot make their own choices are often regarded as enfeebled and in need of sympathy or help. But appearances can be deceptive Daniel leads us into a hidden subversive world: a world where everything is not as it appears at first glance. Although Daniel had to live his life with constant hostility in Babylonian chaos and with others in control it is clear that this life was not a failure in any sense. This second-choice location was an arena of stunning success.

We all have to live as least some of our lives in second-choice worlds. Some of us have to live there all of our lives. If our second-choice world is going to be handled well, the way we approach and engage it will be very important. Our perspective on life as we enter our second-choice world has a significant effect on how we respond to it. If our thinking is underdeveloped, our spirituality shallow, and we have no friends, then second-choice worlds can be particularly painful and problematic. When Daniel arrived in Babylon he appeared to have nothing but it was not long before his wisdom, perception and a close relationship to God started to emerge. What resources was Daniel drawing on which enabled him to deal with this Babylonian and second-choice world?

Grasping the context

*He was to teach them the language and literature
of the Babylonians.* (Daniel 1:4)

Daniel was compelled to learn the ways of Babylon. His second-choice world was insistent about what it required from him. This would have been demanding and difficult but ultimately it was essential. Daniel was going to respond to the opportunities offered in Babylon and this meant that learning its literature, language and culture was pivotal .

If we are going to flourish in our second-choice world we often have to wrestle with, engage with, and eventually understand the sort of Babylon it is. If we are dragged off to live in a world we do not want, our first response will be to resist the circumstances or the people who are doing this to us. Eventually, when the long-term nature of our situation seeps into our thinking, we have to embrace this second-choice world or we will forever live in conflict and perpetual exhaustion. The turmoil of opposing and embracing our second-choice world enables us to understand the nature of the new environment in which we have been placed. This is true particularly in the initial stages of the experience. Just as it is in arguing, loving, playing and talking with our friends that we get to know what sort of people they are, so a similar process takes place when we in encounter second-choice worlds. By living in the whole context of its joy and pain we come to understand our world and how we fit into it.

Second-choice worlds are often intimidating — not least because we prefer not to think about them. When we enter, our lives are full of fear because our second-choice worlds have taken on a monstrous image which has been fed by our ignorance of the surrounding realities. As switching on the light in the bedroom of a frightened child dispels the monsters of the imagination so understanding the nature of our second-choice world frees us from our fear and intimidation.

Daniel and his Hebrew friends got to know Babylon and invested a lot of time, energy and talent in seeking to understand it. It was a totally alien thought-world with a very different God and world-view from the one they had left in Jerusalem. Babylon was a world of gods who were the personification of natural forces, and of a collection of minor deities and demons, all of whom operated in a world of sorcery and astrology.[3] But they could see that the Babylonians valued 'young men, without any physical defect, handsome, showing aptitude for every kind of learning, well informed, quick to understand and qualified to serve in the King's palace'.[4] Yet it was a world that he clearly perceived and eventually understood. Daniel and his friends perceived Babylon well.

There are three environments which we have to perceive and understand if we are going to work well in our second-choice worlds. We have to understand the environment of *our immediate world*, the world where people do not acknowledge God and insist they have no relationship with him. What is the world-view of my contemporary non-Christian friends and how can I relate to them through it? How do people think, decide and live their lives in the place where I have to live my life? We also need to understand the environment of *our Christian community*. How healthy is my local Christian community? Does it know how to remain connected to God and walk with humility? To what extent can I trust my Christian friends in helping me through my second-choice world? To what extent can they trust me? We also need to understand *ourselves*: the nature of how we as individuals interact with the other two realities. All these things are to be held together in dynamic tension. If we do not understand ourselves it will be difficult for us to understand our world. If we do not

---

[3] Goldingay, *Daniel*, p. 16.
[4] Daniel 1:4.

understand our community it will be difficult to understand our place of work or service.

To achieve this we need a particular skill in observation. This is essential if we are to make an accurate estimate of the world in which we have been placed. Christians spend a lot of time listening to God, reading the Bible and hearing sermons. We are not so adept at listening to the place, people and culture where God has called us to live. We are often unable to grasp the nature of the organization in which we work, the culture in which we have been placed or the persons with whom we experience so much difficulty. Daniel did not make that mistake. Second-choice worlds are more manageable if we truly understand them and when we are able to resist making wild guesses about them while deliberately closing our ears and eyes.

Participation in an alternative culture

*The chief officials gave them new names: to
Daniel, the name Belteshazzar; to Hananiah,
Shadrach; to Mishael, Meshach; and to Azariah,
Abednego.* (Daniel 1:7)

Daniel did not have to deal with his second-choice world alone. He was surrounded by a community of Hebrew friends who became an 'alternative' and 'subversive' group. They were a counterweight to the power and might of Babylon. If we have to live through second-choice experiences it helps if we are able go through it with others. It is in the community of others that we are often able to understand the nature of our second-choice world; with others we gain perspective.

All the Hebrews had to undergo a renaming process. This represented the stamp of Babylon being placed on these young men. It would have reminded them of how far they were away from Jerusalem, their first-choice world. The new names were the mark of change and an indication of the inevitability of their new future. There could be no greater demonstration of the dominance of Babylon than the renaming of these Hebrews. Yet through being renamed these young men acquired the identity they needed to really engage with Babylon. It reminded them that they were there together. When Babylon put them all through a three-year training process this seems to have drawn them together rather than torn them apart.

People rarely transform their world alone. Often great reformers have a team of people who put 'feet' to the vision and detail into the strategy. Daniel was not alone, he was in this community of renamed Hebrews who were going to sink or swim together. The Western tendency to live through our problems in independence is a weakness rather than a strength. This community of Hebrews would be pivotal in God's plan to subvert Nebuchadnezzar and bring him into grace.

The team was united in its resolve: they were going to stand together and live through the second-choice world of Babylon. The experience of second-choice worlds can form great relationships and build transformational teams. The very fact that we are in a place we do not want to be confronts us with certain questions. How will we cope? Will we just accept the circumstances and submit? Where is our integrity when our lives have taken a perceived wrong turn? The pressure from Babylon seemed to forge these Hebrews together so that they became an alternative and transformational community.

The way we gather into communities shapes how we handle second-choice worlds. If we just gather around ideas, theology, points of doctrine or abstractions we will find it even more difficult to go through unwelcome encounters. These Hebrews gathered around each other as people and resolved together to take certain actions. They not only got to know Babylon but learned how to respond to it as a community.

Blending compromise, negotiation and spirituality

> *But Daniel resolved not to defile himself with the royal food and wine … Then Daniel said to the guard whom the chief official had appointed over Daniel, Hananiah, Mishael and Azariah, 'Please test your servants for ten days.'*
> (Daniel 1:8, 11, 12)

Daniel's entrance into his second-choice world opened a whole new range of choices. He had to contemplate choices which he could never have anticipated before his world was ripped apart by Nebuchadnezzar. They first presented themselves when Daniel along with his Hebrew friends went through a training process which held the dangers of religious compromise and assimilation but it was this preparation which established them for all the challenges ahead. In these initial encounters with Babylon we see Daniel exercising the kind of wisdom which is demanded in the middle of a life-threatening situation. He found himself — a raw untested foreigner — forced to enter a world of half-truth and political scheming. In the middle of this dangerous confusion he had to make a series of good choices.

Daniel had no precedent to follow and no rule book was supplied for these choices. Should he have taken the name Belteshazzar with its occult roots? Regardless of the rights or wrongs, he did. Should he have made a stand over food? For some reason he said no to the food and thus set up a challenge.[5] Whom should he have negotiated with when he wanted to take a stand over food?

He was negotiating in an unstable political environment but within it he had to learn how to integrate his own agenda into Babylon's while remaining submissive to God. Daniel's reality was that no one could make those choices for him. He and his friends had to choose and decide in the best way possible.

Many second-choice worlds are like this, especially if we come to them after childhood. They are uncharted waters full of cross-currents and whirlpools. We have entered a world that is new and in front of us are many complex choices. I have a friend who is a lawyer in New York and the regular question of his second-choice world is, 'How do I avoid lying today and keep my job?' I have another friend who was very vocal against the remarriage of divorced people. Then his own daughter married a divorcé and he had to encounter his second-choice world through his daughter.

Second-choice worlds become dangerous if we do not work through the process which Daniel had to experience. It is the process of adjustment, the realization that in this world I have to make compromises, know where to be resolute and negotiate with the new reality. The option of insisting that regardless of our change in circumstances we are going to live exactly the way we lived before may

---

[5] Baldwin, *Daniel*, p. 83.

seem attractive and even courageous but could prove to be dangerous. Living in denial of our second-choice world opens up the possibility that it may dominate and finally consume us. We have to face the illness, negotiate with our new and difficult colleague, embrace the challenge of the potential darkness — so that our second-choice world will not snap us in two. Daniel did it well; Babylon did not shatter or snap him. Through his ability to face his new reality he was able to work Babylon into his life and as he succeeded in this so it lost its power over him.

Do what you do well

At the end of the time set by the king to bring them in, the chief official presented them to Nebuchadnezzar. The king talked with them, and he found none equal to Daniel, Hananiah, Mishael and Azariah. (Daniel 1:18–19)

Daniel and his friends threw themselves into this Babylonian second-choice experience. In one way or another they were clearly committed to Babylon. They poured themselves into this experience, even though they did not want to be there and Babylon was all that they might easily have found 'impossible'. They worked so hard and well that they surpassed their Babylonian contemporaries — those for whom Babylon was the first-choice world. The Hebrews demonstrated 'wisdom' and 'understanding' and did it all in the service of an institution and culture which was totally alien to their own. For the Hebrews, 'wisdom' was not just about being smart or clever. It was always associated with godliness and carried the sense of living responsibly before God. These Hebrews gave the very best they had received from God and they gave it to an anti-God community. It is possible that their major drive was to avoid death and the best way to achieve this was to serve enthusiastically, but as the story shows they were ready to face death at any time.

It was a remarkable process and one which challenges all of us. Rather than avoiding or running from their second-choice world they pursued it and gave it their very best. They headed for the centre of the volcano, the heart of the storm, the vortex of all their fears. For these men, the way to face Babylon was to become skilled and powerful insiders — not 'separated' outsiders. When they chose this way they rejected pouting, self-pity, resentment and self-consumption. The fact that Babylon was a place of dislocation, pain and disappointment did not compel them to make a negative response to this pagan world. Being servants of God in Jerusalem or Babylon alike demanded living well before him.

It is very easy for Christians to sidestep this responsibility. The separatist thinking I am referring to goes something like this. Christians perceive themselves as servants of a holy God. Yet they usually find they have to work in an office or factory among people they perceive as godless. They feel that serving this second-choice world is not serving God. The result is a kind of self-fulfilling prophecy. Christians remain the isolated outsiders who look a little strange but pure. Unfortunately, they are not always that pure and are often proud, judgemental and isolated amongst the people for whom they are called to be salt and light. Daniel and his friends embraced the realities of Babylon. They dug deep into the culture and came up with gold.

Chapter Four

Lan's story

I had just come back from a trip to Turkey and had some work to do at home. My wife and our lodger had gone to work when the phone rang. To my considerable surprise, a man on the other end of the line asked, 'Could I talk to the Chinese girl staying at your house?' I told him we had no Chinese girl staying at our house — he must have the wrong number. I returned to my work but after a couple of minutes the phone rang again. It was the same man with the same question. I gave him the same answer but with a little more force. He apologized, saying he was sure he had the right number and I assured him that he was mistaken.

I was in the middle of preparing a paper for a conference and when I am thinking about something I occasionally wander around the top floor of the house. I got up from my desk and drifted across the hall. I decided to go into the spare bedroom so I could look over the valley behind my house. It is not particularly inspirational but it is better than looking at the apartment block out of the window of my office.

I opened the door and there in the bed was a Chinese girl. She sleepily raised her head from the pillow, I quickly apologized for disturbing her, her head hit the pillow, and I closed the door. I was in something approaching a state of shock. Who was she? Where had she come from? How did this guy on the phone know she was living in my house and I did not? Who was he anyhow, this man who knew more about my house than I did? How had this happened? Had she floated down from heaven and landed in my spare room?

I phoned my wife at work and asked her, 'Tell me Sheila, do you know anything about the Chinese girl in the spare bedroom?'

'Oh!,' she replied, 'didn't we tell you about that? All the arrangements were made for Lan to stay while you were in Turkey. She's a friend of Kate's.'

Kate was our lodger; she and my wife had sorted it all out but neglected to tell me. They both agreed it was my fault because I travel so much and they did have a point. So, who was this mystery Chinese girl?

Over the years we have come to know the remarkable story of Lan. She is indeed Chinese but she did not float down from heaven; she comes from Vietnam. At the age of seven Lan and her family found themselves on a boat in the South China Sea, having sold all their possessions and handed over their property to the government, so they could join the group of boats that were heading for Hong Kong and exile. At the time there was a wave of anti-Chinese persecution in Vietnam and Lan's parents knew it was time to make huge sacrifices and go. They must have known that their lives would never be the same again. After a week at sea they landed in Hong Kong, and were placed into transit camps where they had to wait while the bureaucratic process found them a place in the West which would accept them. For Lan and her family that place was England. Once the process was over this seven-year-old girl had gone through one of the most dramatic and traumatic refugee relocations of the late twentieth century.

On her arrival in England Lan was able to adapt quickly to her new surroundings. She was and is very bright. When you talk to her today, twenty years after her South China Sea experience you might think you were talking to someone born and bred in England. In fact Lan speaks English better than many native speakers. She is perceptive and intelligent. When she eventually arrived in the English Midlands there was a family which took particular interest in her. Thanks to their purposeful daughter, who was Lan's friend at school, this English family were able to bring her into their family circle and influence her for good. Their warmth and acceptance enabled Lan to understand the British way of life and thinking; they also provided a safe space for her. Although things went well for Lan during those years of adaptation, the transition experience was very difficult for other members of her family. They have never really recovered from the pain and dislocation of being in their second-choice world.

Lan's teenage years were great. She had all the intelligence, eloquence and social skills to do brilliantly at university and head for London to work in a small publishing company. Like so many in the overseas Chinese community, she climbed the social ladder very quickly. It was in this relocation that the realities of what she was and where she was began to eat away at her confidence. The real battles of Lan's geographic relocation took place fifteen years after the physical event.

Lan has always had to face a certain amount of racism throughout the whole of her life. She has continually been part of a minority community — Chinese in Vietnam, a refugee in Hong Kong and a Vietnamese boat person in England. She has the skills and experience of a survivor; these are skills which minorities pick up in order to manoeuvre themselves around the majority culture and do well. Racism, although present, has not been Lan's greatest problem. Through all her experiences she has been able to adapt herself to her audience and give them what they want. She is a dutiful daughter at home, a dedicated professional at work and the real woman when she is with her friends. Many Asians have this skill but Lan has it in abundance. Yet there is a price to pay for acquiring and developing this skill and the cost is identity. Having to adapt yourself to many audiences can break your life into a series of disconnected fragments which never seem to come together. You can feel that there is no 'you' to come home to; you have to live with the exhaustion of continual performance and adaptation.

When Lan and I talked about her life I assumed at first that in the second-choice world of England her biggest problem would be race. To my surprise I learned that this was not so. The greatest problem she has is one that you can have without geographic dislocation — a sense of profound responsibility for her family. It may well be that migrating across half the globe has intensified her sense of responsibility but what she feels in England she could have easily felt in Vietnam.

Today Lan is a successful professional working for a multi-national corporation. She is the sort of person you want as your friend, the sort of person you could turn to in any crisis knowing she would deliver what she could. She is a brilliant listener, with rare powers of focus on the other person's agenda and after talking with her for just half an hour one is impressed by her depth and maturity.

How has Lan got through the battles of being a refugee, working through her identity and facing the pressures of being responsible for her family and siblings? Lan is crystal clear about the answer. The reason why she has been able to negotiate all the turbulence of her life is what she calls her 'one-to-one' with God. The crux has always been that God is there for her. She is really able to rest in the love of God and know that he will lead her through the bad times because he always has done. She has seen bad things happen and seen God turn those bad things into something good and useful. It is this simple and deep spirituality which is so outstanding about Lan. She is not particularly disciplined in prayer, yet has worked through it all because she has simply walked and talked with Jesus. He, who was an exile himself, fully understands her world when no one else can. While other refugees in England describe the experience as if they were living with a cancer and have found it impossible to experience joy in their second-choice world, Lan has been able to embrace her second choice and live well.

There is no doubt that her considerable gifting and the friends she has developed have played a large part in making her second-choice world a place of fulfilment. Yet she has been sustained and nourished by one simple process: Jesus has talked to Lan and Lan has answered back. The two of them have been doing this for years.

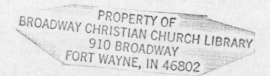

Chapter Five

Fury

The man who concentrates on himself in the
attempt to know himself better and thus,
perhaps, to undertake some moral improvement,
will certainly never encounter God; he will have
to start again, from a totally different angle, if he
wants to find God's will.
(Hans Urs von Balthasar: *Prayer*[1])

This made the king so angry and furious that he
ordered the execution of all the wise men of
Babylon. (Daniel 2:12)

There is a well-known story about an Englishman asking
an Irish farmer, 'Which is the road to Derry?' and being
answered, 'If I was going to Derry I wouldn't start from
here!'

Daniel was 'starting' in Babylon and at the court of
Nebuchadnezzar, so that he inevitably had to continually
work from a place where he 'should not' be. He had to
start each day's journey with what God had delivered to

---

[1] *Prayer*, p. 115.

him. Once he was in his second-choice world there were no new starts; everything was governed — and tainted — by the fact that he was there in the first place. Each phase of Daniel's second-choice world developed from what came before.

Daniel emerged from his initial successful training into a hostile and unstable world. The transition into his second-choice world had been relatively smooth. Nevertheless the culture that intersected Daniel was marked by manipulation, political intrigue and the exercise of power; consequently Daniel was drawn into the political conflicts between Nebuchadnezzar and his astrologers. When the astrologers proved unable to explain the king's dream this opened up the possibilities for Daniel. He had entered his second-choice world on its perimeter but before long, without his consent, he was drawn into the fury of the cultural vortex at its centre and found himself being swept along in it.

I was standing on a platform in Oxford Circus underground station in 1972. I was on my own waiting for another to come. As I stood on my own waiting for the next train I heard a tapping sound. Looking up I saw a blind man tapping his stick along the wall of the platform. He carried a piano accordion in his right hand. As he made his way to the other end of the platform I watched with no particular interest until he attempted to put his accordion down. He stumbled and missed the edge of the platform. The weight of his musical instrument and the momentum of his body combined to tumble him into the pit above which the lines run. I was terrified. I knew that I had to do something; there was no one else to do it. I broke out into an instant sweat and ran down the platform desperately trying to remember which of the three lines below me carried the thousands of volts which made it the potential killer. I jumped down into the pit and grabbed the stunned man. As I did so I heard a faint rumble and felt a breeze. I knew what this meant and the thought that shot through my mind was that 'We're were going to die'. With strength that I never imagined I possessed I took hold of his body and threw him on to the platform. As I did this, a train raced though the *other* tunnel to arrive on the *other* platform. With all my strength gone I crawled up and lay next to the breathless blind man.

What I expected to be a pleasant train ride home had been transformed into a very hostile and life-threatening situation. My normal life had been intersected — as Daniel's was — by circumstances which were beyond my control and I had to respond in one way or another. Second-choice worlds are like that. Sometimes you have to cope with the slow build of tension and difficulty and at other times with the crashing of forces which are furious, turbulent and shocking.

But turbulent times are often times of change and also times of opportunity. Daniel was totally unable to exercise control in this second-choice world. He had to respond to the rapid, unstable and eccentric responses of his boss Nebuchadnezzar in a context which had become one of imminent death. The fact that Nebuchadnezzar could not even remember his dream was doubly ominous, since until the dream could be recalled it remained a threat to the dreamer.[2] Now that Daniel found himself on this particular tiger he had to ride it to the end, whatever that end might be. How did he cope with this unexpected and confusing fury which his second-choice world had thrown at him?

---

[2] J. Baldwin, *Daniel,* p. 88.

Using wisdom and tact

Daniel spoke to him with wisdom and tact.
(Daniel 2:14)

There are many training courses available on how to handle people. Most of them focus on techniques of communication and seek to answer the question: 'How can I get what I want out of this situation or person?' Few begin with any attempt to go beneath the superstructure of communication and deal with the issue of wisdom. We live in an age which values communication techniques above having an adequate root system to our own thinking. This is a disaster. It is destroying us; we are becoming slick, smart and moronic all at the same time.

I remember having a very bad day in the Pacific Coliseum, Vancouver, in 1995. The stadium had been transformed from an ice hockey rink into a conference centre and tickets were not cheap. The team of motivational speakers were a mixture of Christians and non-Christians, and the alliance between the two was revealing. The whole day congealed into two messages: 'You can be what you want to be' and 'If you have faith you can do anything'. Sometimes I was not sure whether I was in a management seminar or a religious convention, but to most of the participants this did not seem to matter because it all amounted to the same thing — get excited, get smart — and you can live a wonderful life if you apply these principles. It was a very bad day: the sort of day that makes me want to go on a long walk after it is over so I can somehow put space between the last experience and the next. Why was it so bad? The speakers slipped past wisdom and on to tactics; they avoided substance and slid to image. I had gone there expecting to look at Marilyn Monroe and all I saw was Frankenstein.

Daniel was good at communication. He responded to the fury of Nebuchadnezzar with consummate tact. He had great technique. But these abilities were rooted in his character and not in his expertise – for Daniel was a wise man. There is no course available which will make us wise. Wisdom does not come fast and it defies any attempt to package it. Wisdom comes from a thousand encounters with things, immense and trivial, which we observe, digest and build into some subconscious whole. People can help us understand how to put it all together but even then it remains stubbornly difficult to package.

In the middle of this ferocious crisis caused by the king's dream and in his second-choice world Daniel had to grasp three things. He needed to know the motivation behind Nebuchadnezzar's irrational order to execute all the 'wise men' of Babylon including Daniel and his friends. He needed to know how much time he had to do what was necessary if they were to survive the crisis. He needed to see if there was any possibility of influencing the agenda.[3]

In order to understand the predicament he was in, Daniel needed to ask questions. He did not merely guess at the way Nebuchadnezzar's mind was working, but got information about the reason for the king's behaviour. In order to handle our second-choice world well we need to be able to ask good questions: that is, questions which when answered will give us what we need to know. There are other kinds of question: Daniel's question was a 'why?' question and not a 'why me?' question, which is something totally different. 'Why?' is a question for understanding. The 'Why me?' question is often merely a reflection of self-absorption.

---

[3] Daniel 2:14–16.

In our second-choice worlds we can quickly slip into a state where self is continuously being at the centre but there is no sense of self-pity in Daniel. Self-pity means that we cannot get the right perspective we need in a crisis.

Daniel negotiated time. When he went to Nebuchadnezzar it was time he asked for — a wise thing to do if you are about to die! Daniel thought that there was a possible solution to this hostility and so he negotiated.[4] He clearly had some sort of relationship with Nebuchadnezzar which enabled him to do this and Daniel's networking skills had already been established. In doing this Daniel was starting to set the agenda for dealing with the crisis. Understanding the fury and making space for a response were crucial in dealing with the problem.

Joining a praying community

Then Daniel returned to his house and explained
the matter to his friends Hananiah, Mishael and
Azariah. He urged them to plead for mercy from
the God of heaven concerning this mystery, so that
he and his friends might not be executed with the
rest of the wise men of Babylon. (Daniel 2:17–18)

This subversive Hebrew community was a community of prayer. Group prayer was central to how they influenced and were influenced by this crisis. After Daniel gained an understanding of what was going on in Babylon he threw himself on God and therefore on the community. This praying community — which had been formed through the pressures and stresses of initiation into Babylon — now

---

[4] Paul was a skilled negotiator. See Acts 22:25–26; 23:1–10.

needed to pray. Flourishing in a second-choice world requires us to develop a community that knows how to pray.

It is in prayer that we are most fully ourselves: people gathered before God responding to their Creator. It is through prayer that we start to engage the large dimensions of our reality, and without it we are destined to live our lives in smallness. It releases the imagination and creativity we need in times of crisis and engagement with our second-choice worlds. Wisdom, understanding and revelation come to us as we submit ourselves to God and allow him to initiate what he will.

Daniel was prepared for God to answer prayer. Prayer does not always bring the answers we want but it does set up the conditions for us to respond to whatever answers we get. Prayer, like most conversations, gives us the perspective to see what is going on even though we cannot control all the circumstances.

If we are going to mature and respond adequately to our second-choice world we need a community alongside us. Such a community needs to be a group of people, many of whom are friends, who are submitted to and in conversation with God. Daniel was a visionary, extremely intelligent, a skilled politician and negotiator — but he still needed to engage with a community in prayer.

Possessing an adequate vision of God

*During the night the mystery was revealed to
Daniel in a vision. Then Daniel praised the God
of heaven.* (Daniel 2:19)

We learn a lot about ourselves in a traffic jam, at airports during flight delays and at most times when we do not get what we want. Second-choice worlds give us the chance to see what is inside us, an opportunity to see what we are really like. It is often the collision of first- and second-choice worlds which cracks open the reality of who we really are. These testing times are very precious times; they are gold dust to someone who wants to live with a measure of self-understanding.

When I first went to India I was twenty-four and felt that I was a nice, calm, relaxed Englishman. I clearly had a lot of learning to do; it turned out that much self-revelation was needed to ease me out of my confident smugness. Crossing cultures has the effect of zipping us open and giving us the chance to look inside. On one occasion it was when I went to get a railway ticket that I had a good look at myself. In England this is a relatively easy task, at least if you speak English. You wait a while and then buy the ticket. Assuming it would be the same in India. I joined the long line of people at the station and waited . . . and waited . . . and waited. I waited two hours and then when I got within six feet of the barrier a shutter came down and my line was closed for the day. Where was the nice calm Englishman? I was in a rage — a wild animal which I did not know I possessed was crashing through my rib cage and letting everybody within earshot know that he was around. So who was to blame for my loss of temper? Was it India? Indian railways? The man behind the counter? Or was it me? To be honest, all Indian railways did for me was show me truth of who I was when I met certain conditions. It was not a pleasant experience but it was a good one. Second-choice worlds do that sort of thing; they get inside and work away at us. Second-choice worlds hold up a mirror to us and ask us to have a good look at what we see.

Daniel had to live through the fury of his second-choice world. We look inside him, and what we see is spectacular.

There is no doubt that he was relieved when he had a revelation from God regarding Nebuchadnezzar's dream; it meant that he was going to live! Daniel 2:19 shows how the released tension triggers an outburst of praise which reveals Daniel's internal world and in particular his vision of God. What do we see in Daniel's prayer of praise?

Praise tumbled out of Daniel. He had a broad perspective on the future and history of God — his nature and everlastingness. He knew that God is for 'ever and ever'. God had revealed the complexities of Nebuchadnezzar's dream and Daniel was overwhelmed. Daniel and all the wise men of Babylon had been locked into a strict time-scale within which they must either understand the dream or face death. The knowledge that God is eternal is crucial in handling second-choice worlds. Inside, Daniel knew that Babylon was temporary and that only his God was eternal. This sort of perspective on time has the power to reframe second-choice worlds.

Daniel praised the 'wisdom' of God. God is able to understand all the dimensions of people's dreams and of their power games. God could see under, over and through the problems presented to Daniel. The riddles and traps of this second-choice world are fully known to God. Daniel praised God for his 'power'. The notion is that Daniel knew God had the ability to do what he wanted to do. Daniel might be living in a second-choice world but in this world too God still operates in strength. God is as powerful in second-choice worlds as he is in first. Daniel praised God because 'he changes times and seasons'. God was in control of Nebuchadnezzar's time and Daniel's time. Daniel was living with the sense that God is in charge of the timing of events. He is Lord of time and the times in between time: the periods when nothing seems to be happening, when we are becalmed and it looks as if there is no wind to take us forward to the destination.

Perhaps most startling is that Daniel was aware of God's ability to perceive darkness. God, said Daniel, 'knows what lies in darkness'. The darkness of Nebuchadnezzar's world was not darkness to God; to him it was as day. This is very important for people who have to live in second-choice worlds. There is no darkness, riddle, mystery, relationship or task which God cannot perceive and respond to adequately. Daniel was celebrating that darkness is not total blackness to God. If darkness is not total blackness to God then there is a chance that we may be able to see what is going on and grasp how to handle our second-choice worlds with all of their inevitable darkness and confusion.

Courage to speak

The king asked Daniel (also called Belteshazzar),
'Are you able to tell me what I saw in my dream
and interpret it?' (Daniel 2:26)

There are periods in our second-choice world which in retrospect can be seen as times of sea change. There are initiatives, conversations and responses which have the power to transform things even though we did not realize it at the time. Daniel went into the presence of Nebuchadnezzar and spoke; Daniel's world was never the same again.

Second-choice worlds can be intimidating; they are often places that can close us down so that we never speak. Occasionally the major players in our second-choice world have a vested interest in hindering us from bringing our thoughts, intuitions or gut feelings to the surface of our lives through speech. There is a reason for this intimidation: it is related to the power of expressed truth. When people speak with truth they fill the spaces around them with meaning. They explain what is and what is not and in doing so create not only conversation but also culture. They may appear to do no more than spit into the wind — but when they do so, surprisingly the wind changes direction.

When Daniel went into the presence of Nebuchadnezzar Babylon was given a message that life would never be the same again. This conversation was in effect an early warning system alerting all who heard that the Jewish slave was on the rise and Babylon was heading for disaster. Of course, Babylon did not know this at the time but that did not change the reality of what was happening. From being the one under pressure and scrutiny Daniel became the one who put others under pressure and scrutiny. From a high-flying slave he became the man who could open up the future of the king and communicate to him. He was an immigrant who became a presidential adviser.

Such transformations can produce a wild-ride sort of nausea but they need to be faced if we are going to live well in our second-choice worlds. Why do we fear death . . . the opinion of others . . . growing old . . . or being perceived as a failure? Daniel teaches us that at the right time we need the courage to address such fears. The challenge is to look at the source of the fury and turmoil in our lives and stare it down. We have to invade our fears with courageous truth-speaking and through doing so plunder their power to intimidate. Daniel did this well and we must learn to do the same if we are going to fulfil what God wants us to do in the places we do not want to be.

Chapter Six

Tony's story

Tony is the sort of person you would want at your party; he engages with people quickly and breaks social ice really well. He has strong opinions about most things, enjoys a good argument and is a rock-solid friend. Aged thirty-something, Tony is a policeman. He really enjoys his first-choice world even though he is right at the point of the stresses and strains of modern life. Tony appears to do his job well and has recently been promoted.

Tony became a Christian through observing the life of another colleague when they both were members of the military police. Reflecting on how his colleague responded to the pressures of his work not only helped Tony see how he should live his life but also how he should respond when, as the years passed, he was overwhelmed by issues of second choice.

Five years ago Tony was with another police officer in a car chasing a suspect. For some reason, when they stopped the car Tony's colleague got out and hit the suspect, unnecessarily and illegally. The suspect made a formal complaint and Tony found himself suddenly thrown from his first-choice world into his second. For Tony's colleagues wanted him to say that nothing had happened. He was under considerable peer pressure from the people who worked most closely with him and who wanted him to lie. Following the complaint there was an enquiry, at which the suspect wanted Tony to tell the truth. Tony searched for a way out of his dilemma but found none. He had to respond to this unexpected and catastrophic turn of events in the best way he could. He decided to tell the truth although he knew he would have to pay a heavy price both on a professional and a personal level.

When Tony's colleagues knew that he was going to tell the truth and thus injure the reputation and professional progress of a fellow officer things started to go wrong. Some of Tony's files went missing so he was not able to do his job effectively. He found grass had been put in his 'In' tray. This may seem an innocent prank but it was full of meaning. In England if you betray someone or inform on them you are said to have 'grassed them up'. Tony's fellow officers were in effect telling him that he was guilty of treachery. This non-verbal message was very powerful. The police community in his station had drawn a circle between insiders and outsiders; Tony was on the outside.

For several months no one would eat with Tony; when the canteen was full he would be left sitting on his own. People used to hiss at him while he walked down the corridor and whistle the theme tune from the film 'Omen' while he was on the police radio. The film is the story of a child who is the incarnation of Satan. It is not going too far to say that Tony was hated by several of the people he worked with. He received little institutional support apart from one female officer who would not allow the abuse to continue when she was on duty.

How did Tony deal with all this? He has a very clear-thinking and great woman by his side and she helped him enormously. He was still inspired by the example of the Christian policeman who had so influenced him in the first place. And he had a group of friends who supported him day by day through their prayer, love and personal contact. Together with all of these he had a personal passion for truth which, when mixed with his streak of stubbornness, meant that he just would not — possibly could not — let everything go. With unclear vision Tony just put his head down like a football player on muddy ground and slogged his way down the pitch towards his goal. He also decided to 'do good' to the people who hated him and this seemed to work. There were no flashes of inspiration, no clever answers, no spectacular miracles. Tony just endured ... and in the end prevailed.

My guess is that our cities need a lot more police like Tony if they are going to remain stable and their people safe. Who knows whether some young officer watched how Tony coped with falling into his second-choice world and has been inspired by what he saw to make similar choices when the pressure is on him?

Chapter Seven

Authority

The world is charged with the grandeur of God.
It will flame out, like shining from shook foil;
It gathers to a greatness, like the ooze of oil
Crushed. Why do men then not reck his rod?
(Gerard Manley Hopkins: *God's Grandeur*)

But there are some Jews whom you have set over
the affairs of the province of Babylon —Shadrach,
Meshach and Abednego — who pay no attention
to you, O king. They neither serve your gods nor
worship the image of gold you have set up.
(Daniel 3:12)

We all have to live much — if not all — of our lives in response to some sort of authority. Sometimes that authority is exercised in a manic fury, as it was in Nebuchadnezzar's dream, while at other times it is more sustained and premeditated as it was for the Hebrews on the plains of Dura. Even if our second-choice world is not political in nature it still can exercise authority over our lives and dominate them.

Different cultures set up different symbols intended to establish authority and dominance. These are among the cultural norms to which one must adhere in order to be regarded as an insider. When I was a boy a few of my friends and I worked this out to our advantage and entertainment. I come from Southport, a town which is in the north of England, a town 18 miles from Liverpool. Every year on the so-called glorious 12th of July hundreds of people would come from Liverpool to celebrate the victories of William of Orange over the Catholics of Ireland. As boys we used to watch these people walk around our town dressed in the costumes of seventeenth-century England and Ireland, waving mock swords, playing whistles and beating drums. We noticed that the visitors favoured the colour orange and did not like green. Green was the colour of Irish Republicanism and the demonstrators were Irish Protestant Unionists. This opened up a wonderful opportunity for us. Most of these 'Orange' Protestants would get seriously drunk after the first parade around town. We developed a simple technique to ensure that when they came out of the pubs we could have the time of our lives. We simply painted big pieces of paper Republican green and waved these at the drunken Protestants; an intoxicating riot inevitably followed. They would lunge after us and try to chase us, swearing in temper and, being drunk, fall to the ground. What power we boys had — and all because the colour green had been filled with meaning and so had the power to trigger deep-rooted responses of tribalism and perceptions of truth.

All cultures have symbols which are the touchstones of orthodoxy and acceptance. Often their power is incomprehensible to outsiders. I find it difficult to understand the relationship of the Americans with their flag and the French with their language. They in turn have difficulty understanding the significance of the royal family to the British. In second-choice worlds we encounter new symbols and new meanings and try to work out what they mean. Daniel and his friends were confronted by a huge image of Nebuchadnezzar on the plain of Dura. Today our second-choice worlds may demand and insist that we pay deference to the gods of sex, money, power, technology, popularity, compromise, ambition and image.

Second-choice worlds can be very insistent in the way they exercise power and control. Nebuchadnezzar felt the need to control his people. If anyone misunderstood or did not conform to his demands this would endanger the whole of the authority structures of Babylon. He had a complex culture to maintain and people who did not submit had to be dealt with harshly. Nebuchadnezzar made it very clear how people should respond to him. His herald was explicit: 'This is what you are commanded to do, O peoples, nations and men of every language.'[1] He went on to state clearly the nature of the musical symbolic actions that were to trigger the response of Nebuchadnezzar's subjects: the right posture of worship and the penalty for non-compliance.

In the West we are constantly under pressure to comply. Not a week goes by without some financial institution telling me that I need to borrow money from them. Magazines for each gender explain what values contemporary men and women should live by. Flick through most of them and you will learn that wealth, sex, image and power are the values of the age and — by implication — that if you don't get on with these then you are stupid, dull and missing out very badly. The tone is generally pushy and authoritative.

---

[1] Daniel 3:4.

Today, in a similar way to Nebuchadnezzar's Babylon, there is a culture that requires people to bow down to its values. Its own sustainability depends, so to speak, on people bowing down and sucking up. The fact that alternatives have to be sidelined, silenced and humiliated is significant. This need to control demonstrates its own fragility; if alternatives were tolerated they might show up the weakness of the whole system and bring it crashing to the ground.

I write these particular lines from just outside St Petersburg, Russia, known from 1918 to 1991 as Leningrad. In 1917 all the hopes of the people were expressed through revolutionary zeal and Russia exploded in violence. Soon the Communists took control and determined to transform — and to dominate — everything. Movement, education, food distribution, thought, values and the all-important concept of political correctness were controlled and directed from the centre. Such were the weaknesses of the philosophy and the system that it could not survive without devastating powers of control and penalty. People who challenged the system, like Sakharov and Solzhenytzin, paid a heavy price for standing out against the powers in control. Yet the price they paid cannot be compared with the millions of lives lost in the whole project of Russian Communism.

Today, things have changed. The penalties are not as harsh; there is more freedom, people are allowed to think as they want but authority is still there. There is no KGB to enforce political doctrine; but now the Russian people are called to respond to the agenda of money, sex and power. Their first-choice world of political freedom has quickly shifted into a second-choice world of poverty and despair.

How can we stand against long-term systematic intimidation from authority? These Hebrews show us a way of doing so in pressures of high intensity.

Clear perspective of who has authority

*Shadrach, Meshach and Abednego replied to the
King, 'O Nebuchadnezzar, we do not need to
defend ourselves before you in this matter.'*
(Daniel 3:17)

The decision of these Hebrews to defy the King and head
for death might appear crazy: lemming-like perhaps.
To be able to abandon themselves in such a way they
had to be stupid or sure of certain realities which seemed
unavailable to Babylon. They grounded themselves in
this reality, which was basically the sense that although
Nebuchadnezzar was in charge of them God was in charge
of him. They were living in a world of authority but the
authority was God's and not Nebuchadnezzar's.

Going through our second-choice world well depends
on understanding who is in charge of the process and who
has allowed us to be there in the first place. It is very difficult
to deal with second-choice worlds if we feel we arrived
there by the fling of some cosmic dice or by the whim of
some powerful person. The shock for Nebuchadnezzar was
that these Hebrews lived under the authority of God and
not of Babylon. It was because they were serving God and
not Nebuchadnezzar that they worked well, served a hostile
state, learned the culture, and took up influential positions
in Babylon. This was the reality that dawned on the king
right at the moment when he felt himself most powerful.

As we live in our second-choice world, the knowledge
that whatever or whoever has been the cause of our entering
it does not possess the final authority over us, is transformational. Sickness does not rule: God does. My boss does
not rule: God does. The majority do not rule: God does.
These are the realities which open the door for grace to

operate in our second-choice world, and it is these realities which toughen us and enable us to stand.

These Babylon-based Hebrews were also living with another kingdom which dominated their lives. Babylon was not their home but Jerusalem. It was the reality of that invisible Jerusalem-based world which shaped the decisions of the second-choice Babylonian one. No wonder they could live with so little attention to themselves.

Leaving the consequences to God

> *But even if he does not, we want you to know*
> *that we will not serve your gods . . .* (Daniel 3:18)

Once we are able to sort out where authority lies in our second-choice world then we can deal with the implications. If we focus only on immediate needs and make them authoritative over us then we will always live as their victims. I had to live through this challenge in a very small way when I first went to India. People told me that I might get sick in India, I might die in India — all of their exhortations were related to my health. Some of my friends reckoned my decision to go was reckless. But from my perspective it never looked that way. India was the obvious conclusion of what I was, what I was feeling, what I thought God was saying to me. India was a wonderful opportunity. In some ways India was my first- and second-choice world all at the same time, yet the consequences that might flow from these realities were down to God who had set the whole thing up in the first place. He had set up the context and I was called to respond.

Certainly there was something reckless about the way these three Hebrews behaved before Nebuchadnezzar's authoritative image; their 'recklessness' depended on their sense that they were in the palm of God's hand and that he was the one who would dispose of their lives as he saw fit. It was that recklessness which opened the community to their message. Their stance against the forces of the culture was the initial tremor which brought the lord of the culture to his knees and Babylon face to face with the Hebrews' God.

Living in this inattentive way brings great power; we are able to live freely and to great effect. In our first-choice — and often self-centred — world we hold on to the consequences. The big questions are 'What will I get out of this?' and 'Will it do me good?' We drive ourselves into ourselves and begin to live narrowly. We are cramped within a small and restrictive space of self; our primary characteristic is constriction. This explains why so many Christians appear to live such weird lives. On the one hand they have a huge God, they live in a world of earth-shattering concepts; and yet they live tight little lives which have no more than an occasional fleeting reference to the God they know. If we proclaim that God owns the world, its past, present and future, but cannot live with some sense of abandon and freedom which follows on from this claim, then we start to live in a split world, the world — to be frank — of hypocrisy, and it eventually shows.

We are so strongly gripped by self-protection, security and success that we often fail to see that God occasionally leads us into second-choice worlds primarily for the sake of others. One mark of God's omnipotence is his ability to do more than one thing at once, and he often demonstrates this in our lives. It is true that he leads us through tough situations for our own sakes but the core of some of our difficulties is that he leads us through second-choice worlds for others. Through the plagues of Egypt God set his people free but also explained himself to the Egyptians. Isaac was near to sacrificial death and it was Abraham to whom God spoke not Isaac. Meshach, Shadrach and Abednego were facing death which was all to do with Babylon, their second-choice world. Being able to live through our second-choice world often requires us to grasp that we are not the point of it: someone or something else is. This is hard work for many of us because we have been brought up in a self-dominated world but this defect does not entitle us to avoid this work if we want to truly engage our worlds of second choice. In times of difficulty, over-attention to ourselves gets in the way of engaging with God's purpose for us.

Allowing God room to work

King Nebuchadnezzar . . . It is my pleasure to tell
you about the miraculous signs and wonders that
the Most High God has performed for me.
(Daniel 4:1-2)

Nebuchadnezzar's interactions with these Hebrews stripped him bare. He tried to exercise control over them but found that he was the one who was being controlled. Through their choices the Hebrews were able to witness to the kingdom which sought to enslave them. The invisibility of their own kingdom and the knowledge that their city had been destroyed did not intimidate them from proclamation.

Their stand on the plains of Dura exposed Babylon to the reality of its own self-obsession. Second-choice worlds are full of surprises, but they can often take a long time to explode. When you end up in a place you did not want to be in you will often see things you never expected. God can unfold things in ways which seem audacious and even out of character. The shocking thing in this story was Nebuchadnezzar's conversion. The fact that he was humbled before God is not the shock but rather it is the method God used. He sent Nebuchadnezzar mad. The king was given an eight-year trial of insanity which nevertheless brought him at last to a place of sanity: the correct positioning of his life before God.

We live well in our second-choice world when we are able to live through mystery. If we need everything explained then we shall find life hard when it is apparently inexplicable. Who can explain a deformed child, a premature death, a failed examination, a betrayal or a failure? Yet it is in the middle of such mystery that God does his work. He often appears to use methods which are totally unexpected. He seems to work agonizingly slowly. Yet it is his work and he does it.

God often brings wonder out of disaster and even out of sin if we give him the space to do it. I have a friend who did not want a child when she was unmarried and sixteen but she went on with her pregnancy and had a daughter. Many years later this daughter is her joy and point of celebration. Something similar can be seen in the story of St Petersburg. The city was built through the abuse and ambition of Peter the Great. After an eighteen-month tour of western Europe he began to build it in 1703, turning a fetid bog into an architectural masterpiece. St Petersburg was a part of a wider project to Westernize and modernize Russia. The cost of Peter's ambition was great; thousands died in the building of the city. Yet today St Petersburg is still a wonderful city, a joy to walk around and view. Thousands of people go there for its splendour and beauty. God is not like Peter the Great, but he does take the disasters which such men perpetrate and make something of them. God takes hold of second-choice worlds and turns them into redemption.

He is able to do this even from a visionary tragedy like St Petersburg. He places his hand on them and over time massages them back into life in spite of human frailty and wickedness. Second-choice worlds are often places drenched in grace, as we will see if we wait around long enough — and watch.

Chapter Eight

Ruth's story

Ruth joined a mission agency in Singapore soon after she had received her Master's degree from Seattle University. A confident, talented extrovert with lots of friends — she was always very popular with people who got close to her. Her walk with God was very real and she bounded with energy and commitment to everything that she put her mind to. She was a delight to know and have as a friend.

Quite soon after she began her job the nature of her new world began to become clear. She had crossed a culture and was facing its new challenges. Accustomed to success, Ruth had joined the leadership team of the mission agency as her first-choice world. However it soon became her second.

The leader she was working for had a number of problems. He seemed to want to control the minor details of her work and life. Due to his own fears and hidden drives it seemed impossible for her boss to know what he was doing and why. He was very talented but had little understanding of how he worked with people. His treatment of Ruth reflected a dark side to his character. He pressured and bullied Ruth, taking out on her the frustrations he was experiencing in his difficult job of leading a team of full-time Christian workers in a complex culture.

At first Ruth was able to laugh off the intimidation, but as time went on this became more and more difficult. In public her boss was talented, godly and exceptionally smooth in all he did. In private he would be unreasonable, lose his temper and shout at her. Ruth, extrovert and gifted, had to go through one of the biggest struggles of her life to survive that time on the team. Although she eventually did survive and even flourish she still felt the need to leave the organization earlier than planned.

There was no transformation for Ruth in her job. Although she prayed and talked with others about this situation there was never any resolution: due to the nature of her boss and the way he controlled all the power in the mission it was impossible for her to talk to him and work things out. Ruth just had to go through the experience and hold on while it lasted. She is now doing a different job in Australia with considerable success.

Crucial to Ruth's survival was her own dogged determination not to let this second-choice world dominate her. She proved to be very resilient throughout her time in Singapore. She had good friends who were able to deflect the attacks on her and help her see them in a different light and she had a great sense of her own future, and — perhaps most importantly — a grasp of her own value. She lived with the firm knowledge that God was for her and so was her family. Second-choice worlds can be survived and even become first-choice worlds with these sorts of resources. Yet the reality of Ruth's experience is that in spite of all her resources and strengths she has not fully recovered from the scarring of those years.

Today Ruth is doing well. She has married, is enjoying her job and about to move to a house she loves. Occasionally she reflects on her time in Singapore and although there are painful memories her mind is dominated by all the good things that happened. Rather than her being eaten up with bitterness — the bitterness is being eaten up by grace.

Chapter Nine

Endurance

*There is a man in your kingdom who has the
spirit of the holy gods in him.*
(Daniel 5:11)

We are all heading for a second-choice world which most
of us want to avoid. It is the world of the old: the time in
our lives when our bodies do not do what we want them
to, and energy is sapped from our frame. Granted, we may
hope to have acquired wisdom and experience to compensate for the loss of vitality but our first choice would be
to have energy, speed of thought and the ability to do
whatever we want.

Daniel was probably in his early eighties when he encountered Belshazzar at the famous — or infamous — banquet
and experienced the disaster which followed. We have the
picture of an ageing civil servant, a long way from home,
working for a hostile power and dreaming of Jerusalem
and how it could be restored. Possibly he considered the
bulk of his life was over so that he could now glide into
some sort of Babylonian retirement. Yet he was not given
the opportunity to retire. The second-choice world which
had dominated him in his youth was still controlling him

in his old age. Daniel's life did not get easier as he got older; at no point did his second-choice world just roll over and submit to him; he had to endure it long into the effects of age. Maturity did not seem to offer Daniel any more choices than he had had in his youth. As we see this old man being summoned to Belshazzar's party and later thrown into Darius' lions' den we are clearly not looking at the picture of an elder statesman who had reached retirement with everything sorted out and under control. Yet Daniel rose to both occasions and handled them well. Even if age had affected his body, his walk with God had not deteriorated. He retained his gifting, vision, courage and perception.

Many of our second-choice worlds require stupendous endurance. Quick-fix solutions rarely solve the most profound problems. Parents age and need to be cared for; personality traits we wish were not ours reappear as we make fools of ourselves yet again, and the body we have had since adolescence is not transformed however many products we may have lavished upon it.

In wealthy countries there is a notion that retirement will sort out my problems. It is there that I will be able to enjoy my first-choice world and all will be well. Then I can travel . . . go fishing . . . fulfil all my dreams on the beaches of Bali or some other distant place in sublime ease. But many people never reach this wonderful world. Sickness, debt, neglect, disappointment with children and all sorts of things we never intended intervene. This is where Daniel reappears and draws us into his life. He had already endured Babylon for a long time. When this second-choice world jerked again he had to respond. How was such a vigorous spirituality and response possible after all the years of enduring second choice?

Supple spirituality

*This man Daniel, whom the king called
Belteshazzar, was found to have a keen mind and
knowledge and understanding, and also the
ability to interpret dreams, explain riddles and
solve difficulties.* (Daniel 5:12)

Belshazzar decided to throw a 'banquet for thousands'.[1]
This was a decision of such outstanding ineptitude that it
leaves me breathless at the thought. Not far from his city
was an army about to come and destroy him and take away
his kingdom but all he could do was party. Belshazzar's
own intelligence systems were apparently unable to relay
to him that he was in the deepest danger of losing everything. His behaviour stands in contrast to Daniel's. Having
lived in obscurity for a while, Daniel was suddenly drawn
into the national vortex again. The queen mother remembered how he had interpreted Nebuchadnezzar's dreams.
Might he also be able to interpret the writing on the wall?
The writing paralysed Belshazzar's team of experts as they
witnessed the hand of God at work; they had no explanation
for the king. This Babylonian culture was coming unglued
very quickly; all the signs of culture disintegration were
there as the panic set in.

Belshazzar and his people were locked into self-
indulgence. Their primary goal being the pursuit of
pleasure,[2] they clearly loved to party. Now I love parties,
and go to as many as possible, but there is a way to party
and a way not to. When it is badly done partying works

---

[1] Daniel 5:1.
[2] Daniel 5:1–4.

against us; Belshazzar shows us how not to do it. Continuous partying for its own sake both makes you dull and dulls you. Endless television watching, persistent drinking and permanent small talk leave their marks on our souls. Pursuits which are intended to inject us with life and joy can often have the opposite effect and in the end stupefy. They have this effect when the only consideration of the partygoer is to squeeze out as much entertainment for self as possible. What should be a celebration of community can slip into self-indulgence and all the potential of the party for soul-building joy has gone.

We live in a party age, self-indulgence is a primary goal: an age when personal first choice seems to dominate everything and everybody. Rather than demonstrating the life of a joyful and relaxed partygoer, self-indulgent partying emphasizes the rigidity and fragility of its participants. Living in a first-choice world where the only thing that matters is a good time for ourselves can prevent us from flexing with the changing circumstances. If we only focus on self-indulgence and aim for continual partying we will not be able to observe either the opportunities or the dangers around us. Daniel was not locked into this self-centred world and was able to see what needed to be seen. Daniel could read the writing on the wall.

Enduring second-choice worlds for a long time can give us the sense of what matters and what does not. The continual stretching and flexing in response to unwanted circumstances develops a suppleness which is often missed by people who always get what they want when they want it. The Babylonians were living in their first-choice world but when God wrote they could not interpret the words. When judgement was at their door they were living in fantasies of power and control. If we don't handle them well, first-choice worlds tend to puff us up and float us off skywards like a balloon — bloated, out of control and unpredictable. This did not happen to Daniel. He flexed with the reality that he perceived around him, responding with appropriate attitude, words and wisdom. Old he may have been but his spirit had the suppleness of an eighteen-year-old athlete's body.

If we want to endure through second-choice worlds we must keep on flexing our spiritual muscle. This will mean engaging new ideas and frames of thinking. It will mean developing new relationships with people who will make us grow — which often means people who do not think like us. In the end it may well be the new ideas and relationships which bring light into the darkness and show us the way out of the gloom of second choice. At the very least they may show us how to make the most out of being where we do not want to be.

Unconcern for status

Then Daniel answered the king, 'You may keep
your gifts for yourself and give the rewards to
someone else. Nevertheless, I will read the
writing for the king and tell him what it means.'
(Daniel 5:17)

Most of us anticipate that prestige and status will come with maturity. But when Belshazzar tried to offer Daniel rewards he initially rejected them out of hand. Daniel was apparently not interested in the rewards offered by this second-choice world; he rejected both the gifts and the status which came with them. Whatever the value system of

Babylon he was able to get along without its approval and affirmation. Daniel drew his sense of status from another source entirely.

It is a startling discovery when we realize that no one owes us anything. Second-choice worlds can build up phantom debts; because we live in a place we do not want to live or have to endure pressures we do not want to endure we start to feel that the world owes us something for all we have been through. Surely the pressure and stress we have endured gives us a right be indulged a little and receive some compensation for all our pain and dislocation? We start to feel we have rights and want to exercise them for our own personal benefit.

I have spent a lot of my life with pastors and missionaries. I have seen them struggle with little money, huge challenges and lots of misunderstanding. To mention one example: missionaries usually have a story to tell when they get home but their experience is that people often do not really want to listen. People listen at first but often only for a couple of minutes and then they give the missionary a welcome back-slap and move on. The status which many people assume missionaries have is just not there in many churches. For the missionary this is a severe test. What do they do when they have been engaged in difficult work in conditions which are often second choice and it appears that no one seems to care?

The truth is that it is not just so-called 'full-time Christian workers' who feel this way. Many others who have suffered long and hard for many years never receive the rewards of praise and acceptance from their own communities. People who permanently struggle with pain, look after sick family members, have to cope with unemployment or find themselves in continual poverty have to deal with a sense that someone owes them something.

Yet Daniel displayed a stark unconcern for Belshazzar's offer. He probably knew it did not mean much anyway in view of the impending collapse of Belshazzar's kingdom but — that apart — it is clear that his status and rewards came from other sources. Daniel knew his status and rewards were built around the Hebrew community of which he was a part: continual communion with God, and the anticipation of a restored Jerusalem.

If we are in a second-choice world and likely we stay there for the long haul then we have to work out where we are going to gain our status and rewards. If we are not able to work this out bitterness and cynicism are there waiting to become our best friends. One of the advantages of second-choice worlds is that they put pressure on us to work out who we really are and where we can safely build substantial foundations for our lives.

Tough integrity

*The administrators and the satraps tried to find
grounds for charges against Daniel in his conduct
of government affairs, but they were unable to do
so. They could find no corruption in him.*
(Daniel 6:4)

Daniel showed an enduring integrity; the continual dependence of Babylon on him emphasizes his trustworthiness. In spite of all the darkness, twists and challenges thrown at him this second-choice world was still relying on him. Daniel was 'neither corrupt or negligent'.[3] He had managed to surf the waves of this second-choice world and

---

[3] Daniel 6:5.

even after all he had been through he was still skilfully negotiating the white water of Babylon.

Second-choice worlds can be worlds of unhelpful or dishonest compromise. Disappointment at not being in our first-choice world can cause us to cut corners. I know of one Christian leader who committed adultery because in his mind this was some sort of compensation for not getting a job he wanted. Another stole money from his company because he felt he should have got promotion and was overlooked. The second-choice worlds set up the compromise of integrity and in our weakness we submit.

People mostly lose their integrity through a thousand small cuts. They do not take a big decision to head off into a world of pretence and deceit; it happens slowly. The pressure of second-choice world is such that we can start to slide into compromise and only we are aware of it. It is possible to get things done by appealing to our boss's vanity, or by telling someone how good they are in order to manipulate them later, or by pretending to be what we are not so that we will be more appealing to the powers over us. It is relatively easy to work our way into a more pleasant position through deceiving someone or using power that is not ours. The problem is that this sort of response to our second-choice world demands payment later on. It is after several years of pretence and compromise that people realize that they cannot trust us. This behaviour pattern we have adopted becomes so ingrained that we cannot see ourselves and we find more and more elaborate ways to cover the nakedness of our own souls. Even though many issues of integrity are culturally discerned, payment for lack of integrity falls due sooner or later in various moments of truth.

Somehow Daniel managed to avoid the lingering death of compromise and held on to the core of what it meant to live for God in a hostile second-choice world.

Rhythmic praying

*Now when Daniel learned that the decree had
been published, he went home to his upstairs
room where the windows opened towards
Jerusalem. Three times a day he got down on his
knees and prayed, giving thanks to his God, just
as he had done before.* (Daniel 6:10)

Some worlds are neither first or second choice, they are no
choice whatsoever. In them our circumstances are such that
we do not have any alternative; the choices have been made
on our behalf and we have to live through them. After
Daniel's wild experience with the partying — and now dead
— Belshazzar, Darius came on the scene. Now it was the
lions' den that awaited the aged Daniel. Yet this was by
now in a way familiar ground to Daniel,[4] the Hebrews had
been this way before. Once more this world insisted on its
agenda and he had to respond.

Coping well with our second-choice world is possible
only if we know something of a life of prayer. Daniel
knew how to pray and his prayer was not just spontaneous
but rhythmic. He prayed three times a day. This meant
that Daniel lived his life with a continuous conversation
with God; he kept company with God and did so regularly.[5]
This rhythmic praying was also in effect a rhythmic
affirmation of his understanding of reality. Daniel knew
that God was in control of this second-choice world and

---

[4] J. Goldingay, *Daniel*, p. 126.
[5] J. Baldwin, *Daniel*, p.129, believes that he would not
normally have been seen during the process of praying and that
any observation of him would have been deliberate.

he was committed to talking to him about it. Daniel's prayer silhouetted him against the culture and the shadow cast was used against him. His prayer was also the expression of his hope. It was towards Jerusalem, his first-choice world, that he prayed — and he did this three times a day.

It is in prayer that we find true perspective on our second-choice worlds. Prayer gives us the ability to see the best we can because talking with God brings him into the panorama of our thoughts. Prayer opens up the full dimensions of human reality. As I read the Psalms what strikes me is the sense of full humanity that they express. There are tears, anger, exaltation, thoughts of revenge, worship, tenderness and confusion; all these are embraced in the life of prayer and praise. Far from being an expression of unreality, prayer draws us into the fully real; it draws us into the knowledge that we are human beings, men and women created in the image of God.

Second-choice worlds are often worlds of pain where we need to express the full dimensions of how we feel before the God who created us. As we talk with him and he talks to us we experience and express what it means to be fully human; we are individuals who, having been created by God, talk to him through our troubles. Second-choice worlds unzip us, but if we let them do so they unzip us before God. We remain wounded, tender and in need: just the sort of people who are ready to witness to God's grace in dens of lions, Daniel types who endure and live boldly whatever happens.

Chapter Ten

Avril's story

I became Len and Avril's pastor in 1978. They had been married for a while but Sheila and I were newly weds. It was on the first afternoon of our five years there in that South London church that I became aware of Len and Avril. Len was a warm-hearted open man with a wicked laugh. Avril had been a teenage bride, snatched up by the discerning and quick-witted Len when she was seventeen. They were raising their own family but their love and concern seemed to have few boundaries. They gave endless hospitality . . . ran people round town . . . gave attention to the weak and frail . . . were tireless in doing what they could to help so that others could live their lives well. All this in spite of the fact that Len suffered from diabetes with all the associated complications. He also had an old war injury, which he was very proud of and which brought him a small government pension.

Six years later when Sheila and I were in Pakistan we were shocked to hear that Len had died and Avril — the former teenage bride with the lively outgoing husband — was now alone. Avril has survived the last fourteen years without Len. She has done more: she has rebuilt her life. As she heads towards her seventies, how has she been able to face the pressure of adjusting to her second-choice world?

Avril's personality gloriously combines two apparently opposing qualities; a tender heart and courage to confront her personal reality. She has faced her initial trauma and the long-term consequences without running away. Avril has always been able to accurately assess the circumstances of her life and access the grace of God in the middle of them. Fourteen years ago she was able to face the loss of her husband even though the sharp pain remained for many years and a certain pain remains today. Her courage and tenderness have been sources of strength which have sustained through some difficult years.

Dogs have played a significant role in Avril's survival. Yes — dogs. This is something which I do not understand very well but it is clear as I watch Avril that her dogs have been very important throughout her path of long-term endurance. Avril loves people and does all she can for them, but you see a different dimension of her love when she is relating to her dog. She is able to look at a dog and connect with it in a deeply compassionate way. I sometimes wonder whether she sees in the animal her own vulnerability and the mutual need attracts. I think there are millions of people like Avril who love and relate to the creatures they are close to. When we see this happening we can see other dimensions of mercy and grace. It is as though God has put these animals close to some of us so that through them he can help us to endure through second-choice worlds. I know very little of this sort of grace myself but Avril clearly does and draws strength from it.

Another important thing about Avril is that she is committed to community. She has been a rock-solid church member and leader for many, many years. Like all churches her church has had its ups and downs but Avril has remained dependable in the middle of it all. She has served her community with dedication, loyalty and passion. She has also maintained important relationships outside the church context which have given her strength and inspiration. If we are to survive and flourish in second-choice worlds it is important not to cut ourselves off from the sources of sustenance and life which God provides. This will often mean developing relationships with people and groups outside the immediate context of the local church.

Avril's life is not a closed system; she lives her life with a large degree of openness. Among other things she is able to embrace the new, and is willing to be persuaded by good arguments. This openness has been pivotal. It has meant that when she lost the earthly focal point of her life she was able to find new sources of help and mercy. God has been able to give her new resources to enable her to cope. This is a gift which often seems to slip away from people through their 'middle' years. In middle age we often perceive our first-choice world as stable and any second-choice world as inevitably unstable. Because Avril has been able to remain open she has been able to respond when things have been both stable and wildly unstable.

I remember a Bible teacher who visited the church when I was pastoring it and who commented on Avril's prayer. It seemed to him from the way she prayed that Avril clearly loved God. On reflection I decided that he was right. A huge part of Avril's protection over all the years without her lover and mate has been that she has loved God. In loving God she has received his energy and life and this has enabled her to carry on through the last decade and a half. She has walked and talked with Jesus, and they have become friends. With that friendship has come the ability not only to endure but also flourish.

PART TWO

Accompanying God in a world of second choice

Chapter Eleven

Trouble

I, Daniel, was troubled in spirit, and the visions
that passed through my mind disturbed me.
(Daniel 7:15)

I remember being told when I was fourteen years old that Christians should not have problems or sickness and if they did, it was because they lacked faith and trust in God. I did not believe it then and I do not now; it is rarely true. This notion about Christians and problems was similar to other bits of homespun spirituality I was responding to at the time, such as: 'Christians don't need entertainment because they have Jesus', and an insistence that when truly godly people wake up in the morning 'their first thought should be Jesus'. I failed on all counts but it seemed that God could cope with that better than some of my Christian friends. I enjoyed watching films, playing sport, and my first thoughts in the morning were usually about how I could get a cup of tea as soon as possible. Jesus was rarely my first thought of the day. Unfortunately I have known a lot of people over many years who have believed that trouble, bad patches and difficult moments are judgement: they are God's way of getting even. God does exercise his judgement over us but it is not vindictive or outside his grace and love; with him there is no such thing as pay-back time, no cuffing around the ear just to let you know who is in charge.

Christians are intended to head for trouble and not merely, as they so often do, to judge their lives negatively if problems come along. What kinds of trouble are we talking about? Christians interact with a long list of witnesses: godly people who got themselves into all sorts of trouble because they lived realistically with God. From Stephen to the martyrs of today great Christians have looked at the dislocated world they live in and have decided to pray and . work for transformation. The net result for most of them is trouble of one form or another. Stress, sleeplessness, misunderstanding, pain and criticism are all part of living well for God. In the words of George Verwer, 'If you are not being criticized it means you probably aren't doing anything.' Trouble and engagement with a world of need go together. In the Western world we are being hemmed in by our desire to avoid pain and difficulty. The resulting narrowness cramps creativity and produces a church that is understimulated and bored. Daniel had his fair share of trouble in his Babylonian second-choice world yet it is a world of stimulation and continual challenge. It seems unlikely that Daniel was bored in Babylon.

Problem God

*I, Daniel, was deeply troubled by my thoughts,
and my face turned pale, but I kept the matter to
myself.* (Daniel 7:28)

In the Western world we tend to like our heroes full of positive thoughts, desires and goals. We want our role models, who are able to transcend the mundane and can live extraordinary lives. There is no doubt that Daniel lived an extraordinary life but much of it was mundane. There was little glamour or glitz in being Daniel. At times he was disturbed, drained and isolated. The visions and thoughts that God was giving Daniel were difficult to grasp and understand. Daniel had significant problems. He had to live his life in relationship to those problems because many of them were not going to go away.

You would think that Daniel already had enough difficulties in his relationship with Babylon and Nebuchadnezzar; yet most of his feelings of terror and shock came not from his second-choice Babylonian world but directly from God. Daniel had to respond to the visions that God was giving him; they seemed more problematic than anything Babylon was able to do to him. Daniel's dilemma was not that Babylon was a problem: it was that God was a problem. Daniel's visions were given by God. It was God who spoke to Daniel through disturbing and destabilizing encounters. God's revelations caused Daniel to be 'appalled',[1] and 'trembling'.[2]

God can be tough when the need arises. It can be really difficult when we learn that the one responsible for placing us in this second-choice world is God. He is the cause of the trouble; the whole thing is God's idea. This is particularly difficult when we have no idea of any reason why.

I am reminded of Alan Exley. How can I explain Alan Exley to you? He dug ditches for the local water authority in my home town, drank a lot of beer, was my widowed mother's lover, the father of my brother's friend . . . and he was a man I despised. My mother used to bring him home

---

[1] Daniel 8:27.
[2] Daniel 10:11.

from some bar or other in town and both of them would come in very drunk. I watched him slur his words, stumble across the kitchen, slump against the wall and eventually climb the stairs when he thought my brother and I were not looking. Strangely, it was not his drunkenness that I despised: it was his weakness. Adolescent boys are not noted for their capacity to understand and forgive and I was not an exception. Yet, I have no excuses and I seek for none. My feelings for Alan were mostly dark and revengeful. I had been a Christian for a year but I had no grace in my heart towards him. I could not understand how my mother could bear his presence. He was a man living in shadows, empty and ghost-like. My relationship with Alan ended when I was fourteen and I asked what his wife thought about him staying at our house. My mother was furious with me but Alan was more or less gone from my life.

Yet Alan has been a help to me. In a surprising way he has opened up for me all that I did not want to be. For me Alan became the anti-type of what it was to be a man, and I look back on knowing him with a sense of regret rather than anger. For all of his weakness, duplicity and stupidity Alan was just a man like millions of others. He represents for me the measure of the grace of God. If God can love, embrace and work with the Alan Exleys of this world then his grace is great, greater than I know. I got a vision from Alan, a vision of how the world should not be and that can be as powerful as a vision of how things can be.

Living with a sense of purpose is central to being able to deal with the Alan Exleys of our lives. This does not mean that we always see things clearly; it does mean that we can live with an expectation that God is doing something profound in us regardless of whether we can explain what it is. We cannot see what God sees; our perspective is rooted in our own, often restricted, lives; yet God sees it all. Because he sees things as they really are, he can see what we need to experience and respond to.

The fact that Daniel was in trouble was not a problem to God. God had a purpose in mind and he was revealing it to Daniel. The whole experience was not a chance event like a lottery; it was a designed response from God in relationship to the needs of his people. Revelation and distress often come together, however little we like it. The Daniel story tells us that there is an answer to the question of why we go through our second-choice worlds even though we may not see it clearly at the time.

Deep mystery

I was appalled by the vision; it was beyond understanding. (Daniel 8:27)

Daniel was in a fog, he could not see through the almost total darkness. This sure man of faith, who was able to face hostile kings and lions alike, had little idea why God said what he said and did what he did. God was leading him through mystery. Daniel was so desperate for understanding in the middle of the mystery that he pleaded for answers but even when he had the explanations this did not help him feel any better: it rather compounded the problem.[3] Sometimes we should be very grateful when God says nothing.

Often, the more truth we encounter the more mystery we feel. When God moves us on to new areas of work and revelation there is usually a cloud of mystery surrounding

---

[3] Daniel 7:28.

the process. If in our second-choice world we feel we can explain all that is going on around us, it probably means that we have still some way to go in perceiving its real nature. The fact that we 'have an answer' to a problem can mean that we just do not understand the problem. Yet the presence of mystery does not mean the absence of God; often it indicates the opposite.

Like my own inner world, second-choice worlds are often places of mystery. I do a lot of preaching, and sometimes I am shocked by the feelings I can generate inside myself: feelings of anger, frustration and passion. Often the things I am talking about at the time don't deserve such strong feelings but out they come anyway. I have watched this happen in myself over a number of years and after some time I think I have an idea of what is taking place. These feelings are the lava under the crust of my skin, placed there through the events of my childhood. I preach about the betrayal of Jesus or our betrayals of each other and remember a duck, a silly duck, a present which my brother gave me and which I rejected. I preach of shame and I remember trying to keep my school friends out of my house because of its chaos and poverty. Events I thought did not matter come bursting through in volcanic feelings at times when what I am doing does not appear to bear any relationship to my feelings. Thirty years after the event I am still working towards a partial understanding of the influence of rejected ducks, chaos, and poverty and how I react to it all.

Second-choice worlds are often places of mystery. They are dark woods filled with strangers who keep stalking or startling us. Yet they are not worlds without grace and light. When we see the strangers we are able to bring them to the light of God and see how they stand up to the brightness and glory of his presence. They then usually go in one of three directions: either they disappear never to be seen again, their bogus character revealed; or they hang around pretending to have strength which they have lost; or they remain but get transformed into resources of strength and grace. These strangers can get born again.

Answered prayer

Your words were heard, and I have come in
response to them. (Daniel 10:12)

Daniel knew how to pray. In the middle of his trouble he threw himself into desperate prayer, 'O Lord, listen! O Lord, forgive! O Lord, hear and act.'[4] Mercifully, the Lord responded to his prayer.

Second-choice worlds can do wonders for our communion with God but only if we so choose. For they can also sever all realistic conversation with God, leaving us deaf and dumb in relationship to him. There is a pattern of desperate praying which takes place today as it did in the day of Daniel. Daniel called to God out of his desperation; God heard and sent his servant in response. Daniel responded honestly and was then strengthened by the servant of God.[5] This strength came through assurances that there was no need to fear and that Daniel was highly esteemed; and also through the touch of the man from God. God was with Daniel in his difficulties, giving him encounter and relationship through the turbulence of second choice.

At this point Daniel discovered that he was a player in a much bigger game than he could possibly know. There were

---

[4] Daniel 9:19.
[5] Daniel 10:7–11:1.

cosmic powers at work in this story, events and intentions which were much bigger than Daniel could conceive. There was warfare taking place in the cosmos, resistance to the rule of God. Like the children who walked up to the wardrobe in C. S. Lewis's *Narnia*, opened it and stepped inside, we, like Daniel, may discover a whole new world which is more real and meaningful than the one we have just left.

Prayer has that magnificent two-fold effect. Through prayer our soul is sustained and restored; through prayer we are able to see that things are much bigger than we first imagined. Prayer leads us from the potential self-centredness of our second-choice worlds, gives us inner strength and prepares us for fresh revelation.

Good friendships show us how prayer works. Spending time with our friends restructures and renews our inner world and gives us perspective on the problems we face. Prayer is answered not only through God doing certain things for us but when we discover that he is our friend. Like a friend, he restores our soul and gives us perspective on our answered or unanswered questions.

Chapter Twelve

Frank's story

I first met Frank when I was in the Sudan in the mid-eighties. He was a little different from most people. He was in Sudan, a long way from his home in Germany, because he and a friend were trying to sort out an educational project for another African country. I was giving a series of Bible studies and Frank sat in on them. He made the Bible studies very difficult for me. The problem was not lack of engagement but Frank's absolute focus on all that was going on. Most people were sitting around responding politely to what I was saying — but not Frank. He hung on every word, story and point. He was so focused he became the focus, his response to what I was saying became what was being said in the meeting, his reactions dominated the room. He did not do this deliberately — it just happened. I told some stories, which in most company are received with occasional smiles and a little laughter. Frank did not smile at those stories — he roared with laughter. I would make a point and he would 'ohh!' and 'ahh!' over it, looking around to the group to catch their response to the point I had just made and smiling when he did so. For the first time in my teaching and preaching career I was thinking of ways in which I could be boring so that Frank would not be so stimulated. I should not have bothered;

Frank engaged anyway and drew us all into his world of response.

I have met Frank several times since those days and he still does the same thing. So focused. So enthusiastic — yet he is always getting into some sort of trouble. After watching him over a number of years it is clear to me that the main reason why he is often in trouble is because he cares. He is not concerned to live in any 'first-choice world'; what he cares about is the state of the world, the call of Jesus on his life, the poverty of spirit in many cultures and how the church so often fails to respond to that spirit. He does not care about his image, money and living a comfortable life, even though most of his friends wish he would give more attention to those areas.

There is fearlessness about Frank. Maybe it is because of the things he does not care about that he is able to live so freely and fearlessly. He is the sort of person you would want with you if you were lost, up a mountain in a foreign country and the dark sky was closing in. He would not be great at the practical survival skills but he would be fantastic company. He has been through so many scrapes, adventures and challenges that you would know being up a mountain with him was just another story he would add to his growing portfolio of exciting stories.

Frank gets into trouble a lot because of his relationship with God. He is so convinced of the call of God to bring the good news of the kingdom of God to a needy world that he will do whatever it takes to do that. He is not stupid or insensitive in all this but he is committed. He does not appear to consider his personal safety that much; he just plunges in and seems to push the angels out of the way in the process. He lives a full life in all of its dimensions, making waves of compassion and sense wherever he goes.

Frank's instincts and responses stand out in contrast to our safe Western world. He gets into trouble because he cares deeply and in this he lives his life to the full. When Frank sits down and tells his grandchildren stories, they will not need to be tales which he learned from other people's experiences and books. Frank will be able to fill the conversation with his own tales of life, death, courage, love and adventure. What privileged grandchildren he will have.

Chapter Thirteen

Eloquence

Lord, Thou art fullness, I am emptiness;
Yet hear my heart speak in speechlessness
Extolling Thine unuttered loveliness.
     (Christina Rossetti: from *Lord, Thou art fullness*)

While I was speaking and praying, confessing my
sin and the sin of my people Israel and making
my request to the Lord my God for his holy hill
— while I was still in prayer, Gabriel, the man I
had seen in the earlier vision, came to me in swift
flight about the time of the evening sacrifice.
     (Daniel 9:20–21)

Daniel's second-choice world offered him the opportunity to communicate significant thoughts. Through his dislocation he gained his eloquence[1] and delivered his messages

---

[1] I am giving the word eloquence an added meaning. In the sense I am using it, 'eloquence' is not just to do with the ability to speak, but is the ability to communicate something worthwhile and significant.

in 'effectual language'.[2] His second-choice world gave him the ability to articulate something of outstanding value. It is likely that he could speak well before all of the events in Babylon; but through his visions, insights and prayer he now had something significant to say. Many centuries after Daniel spoke to kings, interpreted their dreams and saw shocking yet important visions, we still find it worthwhile to seek to interpret what he had to say and the way he said it. Second-choice worlds can give you this sort of eloquence, effectual yet significant speech.

It is easy to send out vocal sounds to other humans and be perceived as an eloquent person and yet say nothing of value. Sheila and I spent some time with certain acquaintances, who we hoped might become friends. We invited them around for coffee, and all we did was listen to them. We spent four hours with them and I think Sheila and I talked for five or ten minutes during the whole time. In the end their conversation was like wallpaper or supermarket music; they created a backdrop to your thoughts but there was no real engagement with them as people. Although they knew how to make sounds there was no real eloquence, no expression or articulation of anything other than a series of incidents in their lives. The fact that the many incidents they referred to had little or no meaning to us did not hinder our guests. They did not want conversation: they wanted to talk. After all those hours of conversation we knew them no better than when we greeted them at the door. I am sure there was more to those people than what they revealed that night but it remained unseen and unheard, in spite, or perhaps because of, their avalanche of words.

---

[2] Chambers 21st Century Dictionary (1996), p. 427.

Speech and pain

Daniel had a dream, and visions passed through his mind as he was lying on his bed. He wrote down the substance of his dream. (Daniel 7:1)

When Daniel spoke an eloquent message to Babylon he told them of his visions and dreams. They were his message not only to Babylon but to the Hebrews and the world; yet they were messages out of pain and dislocation. The experiences of his second-choice world gave his life its articulation; his eloquence was grounded in them. Something similar happened to John the Baptist. He had to live and carry out his ministry in the desert, but for him it was not just a place to live or a location for sleep. Out of the desert came the man with his message. The wilderness he had to inhabit illustrated to him the nature of his own life; God gave him through it a metaphor for all he was to do. John had to see the valleys filled and the mountains flattened in preparation for Jesus, as prophesied in Isaiah.[3] Consequently he lived in a desert and this was an illustration of all that was happening around him. Second-choice worlds can have the same effect. The nature of them is so influential that passing through them does not only teach us what we need to know: they give us a vision, an insight into what we should do and what we should say for the rest of our lives.

This truth can be seen in one of the great film classics. Made in 1942, 'Casablanca' is a powerful and wide-ranging wartime tale, staring Humphrey Bogart and Ingrid Bergman. Bogart played the sharp and cynical Rick

---

[3] Isaiah 40:3–5 and Matthew 3:1–3.

running his bar in wartime Casablanca. The film hinges around his decisions and his behaviour. He can either choose fulfilment and go off with the married Bergman, who is deeply in love with him — or will he make decisions which are related to the bigger issues which wartime throws up? One reason why the film holds viewers so well is that we are not sure about the character of Rick. Is he just a cynical night-club owner out for himself or can he transcend his little life and make a great decision? In the end he decides that individual problems do not amount to a 'row of beans' in comparison to the world-shaking events happening around them. He chooses to let Bergman leave with her husband so they can continue their fight against Nazism.

Finally the film portrays Rick's being able to transcend the small world of a self-centred night-club owner. At first he appears tough but selfish and petty, yet his stature grows as he chooses a second-choice world: a life without the woman he loved. The pressures of his wartime world enabled him to express something of himself that may not have been seen in other circumstances. In this he speaks with eloquence. From his second-choice world Rick tells us that we cannot live narrowly and selfishly when there are bigger issues to face. The defeat of Nazism was even more important than his love for another man's wife.

When we interact with our second-choice worlds in submission to God's purposes we are able to observe our lives appropriately. I would not have chosen sickness in Bihar Sharif, India, in 1976 but the whole experience opened up an entirely new world to me. At the time I had no idea that the three days of vomiting, several days of being unwell and feelings of terror in the back of a Bihar State bus were all part of God's purpose in giving me eloquence. I could speak well before. But the focus was narrow. Through that experience I was able to see the world in a new way and the passion for world mission was set aflame. I had been church planting in Manchester and my vision was so small that I might as well have believed that the world ended within a forty-five minute drive of my fellowship. Through all the initial pain of India God reorganized my life and world-view. I now realized that I had to consider the eight hundred million people of India and add to that the rest of the world. Christians have to engage the world, all of it, if we are going to live as God intended. For Daniel, his second-choice Babylonian world gave him the same sort of eloquence.

Dislocation and focus

O my God, do not delay, because your city and
your people bear your Name. (Daniel 9:19)

Daniel continued to struggle with his dislocation. God was not moving fast enough for Daniel so he poured out his thoughts in prayer. Daniel had to learn that second-choice worlds can give us perception and for that reason God takes us through them at his own pace. When we are closed down in one area we are able to perceive with greater clarity other surrounding realities. Second-choice worlds can help us to observe our lives well and our eloquence emerges from this clearer focus. People who are blind can develop new capacity in hearing and people who have little money often have a greater sense of community than the wealthy. If it is mingled with grace, deprivation can develop new ways of seeing our world.

Daniel was concerned because he was conscious of difficulties for which God was apparently not supplying solutions. One of the trends in the modern world is to respond to our difficulties by overloading our lives with solutions. How can we get this or that which will solve our problems? Wherever we look, we are offered a whole series of solutions claiming to show how we can cope with our personal inadequacy and deal with our specific problems, real or imagined. Often, even when we are not inadequate, people want to make us feel that we are — why else are we bombarded with solutions for baldness, crooked noses, fat thighs and tiny legs?

There is a similar culture in the church today. It is not as aggressive as its secular counterpart but it exists. If there is a problem we need someone or something to sort it out. We tend to judge our pastors and leaders by how well they do this. We want our leaders to come up with solutions rather like those slick talk-show hosts who skate over very complex problems before ending the programme with the simplest of solutions. Yet in our drive for solutions to all our second-choice world problems we can miss the opportunities they bring. We are often so focused on getting out of our problems that we fail to see what is going on in the middle of them.

Eloquence — the ability to say something of significance — can emerge from the concentrated and intent focus which deprivation is able to bring. When every one of our needs is met we can easily slip into a world of silence, a world where we have nothing to say and we simply become consumed in speechlessness. Possessing everything you want all the time produces spiritual numbness. This in turn facilitates a slow but pleasant enough death. Daniel was in his world of dislocation and deprivation. Yet this was the world where he was able to see certain things very clearly. He was fully alive and had something to say.

Daniel had a passion for Jerusalem and the restoration of the kingdom of God. His visions brought him the pain of seeing restoration take place and hearing what God was saying about how this would happen. The fact that he could not see everything clearly and that much of what was going on around him was mysterious did not prevent him from seeing certain things with clarity. He felt the pain, saw clearly and spoke the word of God to his world.

Chapter Fourteen

Jonathan and Margit's story

It was in September 1976 at a conference in Leuven, Belgium, that I first became aware of Jonathan. I was just joining Operation Mobilisation and he was one of the leaders. What struck me about him was his focus and strength. He appeared to be something of a Presidential Chief of Staff; he was aware of everything, had the world at his fingertips and was a constant source of information and inspiration. Jonathan was late to bed and up early to do his work in world mission, which he accomplished with verve and utter dedication. He struck me as the sort of person who I would want with me if ever I got the notion to climb Mount Everest. He would be the one who knew how to find the resources and would answer all of the 'how' questions. He would be the one who would deliver.

Several years later I met Jonathan again, greatly changed. While travelling through Spain his vehicle had swerved off the road in the middle of the night and he was paralysed from the middle of his chest down. This was a different Jonathan. The trauma of paralysis had left him apparently less focused; the sharpness was gone and he was wheelchair bound. Initially, it was hard to see Jonathan in his wheelchair but before long it was clear that he was still communicating but in a new way. Thankfully a lot of the sharpness returned with the passage of time.

Over the years Jonathan has been able to manage his life with the help of Margit, his wonderful wife, and the support of a great family. Watching them has always has been inspirational to me. Jonathan and I shared a room in a conference centre in Atlanta. I got to know him better as we went through the daily ritual of what paralysis means for Jonathan: exhaustion, tedious daily ritual and deep frustration with a body which was not doing what it should do. We also had a lot of laughs occasioned by his incredibly undisciplined hair, which after a night's sleep looked as though it had been constructed by a hairdressing punk rocker.

Jonathan, in the middle of his physical deprivation, lives an inspirational life for all who want to observe. He speaks wisdom even without saying a word. The way he has handled his life and its new direction has been a wonder to me. He still travels the world preaching, teaching and mentoring. He runs World Partners, an organization for former missionaries, and he focuses much of his life on the spiritual needs of disabled people worldwide.

Life is not easy for Jonathan and Margit. Jonathan's recent experience in a 'Stryker' frame must have been agony. Being suspended horizontally for a long period to assist healing is beyond my capacity to imagine. Yet Jonathan's no-choice world has given him, and his wife Margit, clarity and a sense of proportion to people like me. It is easy for able-bodied people to be sentimental about the disabled, to overstate their contribution in some attempt to balance out the inequality of it all. I am aware of that but let me state that from out of this broken body speaks a giant who is all man, tough, resilient, wise, inspirational and eloquent.

Out of significant deprivation Jonathan speaks with total clarity. What does he tell us?

God is able to take people with broken bodies and use them in a way which changes the world. Jonathan may be wheelchair bound but that does not prevent him from being influential in many initiatives throughout the globe. He has been a highly visual illustration of what God can do through disability. Most people's disabilities are not so clearly seen as Jonathan's so they can hide and pretend that all is well. Jonathan's life seems to say: here I am with all my clear weakness and here is God speaking through me to a needy world. Jonathan is one of the clearest messages that God takes hold of weakness and transforms it into strength.

God also speaks powerfully through the marriage of Jonathan and Margit. They have shared the intensity of the last years. I write at a time when things are not easy for them. Jonathan has an infection in an open wound, which will not go away, but he and Margit go through this together. It is an excruciatingly hard time. There is no slick answer for them; other marriages would not have made the distance but they are going through this, by God's grace and strength, together.

Chapter Fifteen

Future

> . . . because he had come to the conclusion that
> to tell the history of anything was, if you did it
> thoroughly and accurately, to end up telling the
> history of everything.
> (Frederick Buechner: *The Storm*[1])

> *As for you, go your way till the end.*
> (Daniel 12:13)

Mary, in her early twenties, wanted to join a team of Christian workers. But she had a problem, which she shared with the team leader Liz. If she joined, would there be any people in the organization of — unlike Liz, she implied — her own age? Liz was herself just twenty-nine years old. Each of us has a future which is tumbling towards us very fast with what appears to be increasing speed. Generations are being squeezed together as never before; time is being crushed.

Living well in our second-choice world depends very much on a sense of timing and on our awareness of time. We need to live with knowledge of the seasons in our lives

---

[1] F. Buechner, 1998, p. 61.

and the season our whole life is in. We all experience phases of difficulty, but some of us live the whole of our lives through a bad period in history. Being a Jew in Hitler's Germany during the 1930s was an horrific experience. The times were dreadful and nothing was going to change until Nazism was defeated. Understanding the period of time we are living through is important if we are to successfully negotiate the realities of our second-choice worlds.

While we need an adequate sense of the time we are living in we also need an adequate sense of future. The way we understand our future radically shapes how we live in the present. Suicide is a statement about the future; it says that there is no way out of my second- or no-choice world other than death. Suicide expresses my decision to make my own future and work my own way out of the confusion I am in.[2] If on the other hand we can see some way out of — or through — our second-choice world our relationship to it can be transformed. We can move on from depression or despair.

Daniel lived with God in multiple contexts which overlapped and interacted with each other; it was no wonder that he was occasionally confused. He had to live in relationship to his past: all the memories and events of Jerusalem, and in relationship to his hopes and dreams about the future. Through it all he had his exhausting, exhilarating, turbulent, visionary life as a Babylonian civil servant. Daniel had to cope with his past, when he became an exile with all its trauma: the present reality in Babylon, his second-choice world; and the future of Jerusalem — with whatever else God was planning.

---

[2] I am aware that there are many reasons why people do take their own lives and that this statement is a broad generalization.

For many today the future is no less complex. We make our prayers, wishes and guesses regarding the future but we really do not know how it is all going to work out. Yet, however great our ignorance, to be able to walk with God in our second-choice world and do it well, we need a sense of the length and breadth of our lives. We need a sense of who we are and the time in which we live.

Daniel appears to have been living with two big ideas about the future, which seem to have dominated his conversation with God in his second-choice world.

Going home

I, Daniel, understood from the Scriptures,
according to the word of the Lord given to
Jeremiah the prophet, that the desolation of
Jerusalem would last seventy years. (Daniel 9:2)

Daniel lived his life in awareness of two futures, one immediate and the other distant. First, he lived with hope for what would happen in his lifetime; but he also had a vision for the eternal purposes of God. These two aspects of his relationship with his future intermingled and seem to have shaped much of his response to this second-choice world. Living well in our second-choice world insists on such an intermingling.

Daniel's main concern seemed to be how he could gain an understanding of the future of Jerusalem. Even though Daniel lived, influenced and led in Babylon, he still longed to go home and see Jerusalem restored. Jerusalem was his home and the city of God. It was where he wanted to be; Jerusalem was his first-choice world. How could life be breathed into his first-choice world so his people could return there? This was so central for Daniel that he pleaded with God in prayer and petition, fasting and clothed in sackcloth and ashes.[3] He was desperate about Jerusalem and how his people could be reunited with his city; his heart was broken over the place he loved.

I have a friend who dislikes London. His best moments in the city occur when he is safely on the train leaving it behind. He sees London as huge, traffic-ridden and dirty. My feelings are totally different. For me it is a city of culture, excitement, and a great place to live. I have come to love London and for me it is home. It is a miracle to me that it works — not perfectly but it does work for many of the people who live there. Although I travel to various places around the world it is always great to come back home. Living in London is definitely part of living in my first-choice world; it is a gift of God to me. London is a place of security, restoration and encounter with God — at least for me. I know one day I will leave it but I will do so with a sense of thankfulness that I was able to live for so many years in one of the world's great cities.

Daniel will have felt much the same about Jerusalem but in a much more profound way. Jerusalem was the place where the Hebrews encountered God. When Daniel thought of Jerusalem he engaged his future and his future was at the centre of his dreams. The notion of getting back to his first-choice world gave him hope for the future. Even though God could use him in his place of second choice, the orientating centre of his life was home. In Jerusalem home and future were wrapped together as the place of encounter with God.

My feelings about London are trivial when placed alongside the story of Brian Keenan. Location mattered to him.

---

[3] Daniel 9:3.

He went to teach in Beirut during 1985 for a change of scene from Belfast. He was kidnapped by a fundamentalist group and was held for four and a half years. In his stunning book, *An Evil Cradling*, he takes us through the trauma and turmoil of his time in horrific darkness during his isolation. In his book he not only tells us the events of his world but also bravely reveals himself so that we can see the state of his life during his detention. Keenan describes what it is like to be where we do not want to be during a time when all hope of the future seemed lost:

> I have been and seen the nightmare exploding in the darkness. I am the charnel house of history, I am ashes upon the wind, a screaming moment of agony and rapture. I have ceased being. I have ceased becoming. Even banging my body against the wall does not retrieve me to myself. I am alone, naked in the desert. Its vast expanse of nothingness surrounds me. I am where no other thing is or can be. Only the desert howling and echoing. There is no warming. I am the moment between extremes. I feel scorching heat upon my skin and feel the freeze of night cut me to the bone, yet I also feel empty and insensible.[4]

Keenan gives us the sense of being in a horrific, no-choice world and it is, at least for that moment, a world without a future.

Our modern world is focused on the now; for many the only thing that matters is the immediate. This means that life is sustainable as long as we are living in our first-choice world; we get what we want and we get it now. Everything starts to unravel when we enter our second-choice world and immediate gratification is denied. It is then that our

---

[4] B. Keenan, 1992, p. 67.

inadequate vision of the future is seen to be crucially important. It was, in reality, crucial all the time but we realize this only when our second-choice world comes along. Without a sense of future your ability to flourish through your second-choice world withers and dies.

Open space

While I was still in prayer, Gabriel, the man I had
seen in the earlier vision, came to me in swift
flight about the time of the evening sacrifice.
(Daniel 9:21)

Daniel lived in a huge imaginative world where God spoke in images, visions and dreams. The rationalism and activism which is the mark of so much evangelicalism today did not trap Daniel; he lived with the immediacy of the celestial world[5] and in rich encounter with God. We can see that he was linked to other reality besides his Babylonian second-choice world. God talked to him and he talked to God and the experience for Daniel was stunning. Daniel was on the edge of revelation — dreaming dreams and seeing visions which staggered his imagination and still stagger ours.

What Daniel discovered though his conversation with God was that the world was much bigger than his second-choice world. There were other realities which the politics, vendettas and intrigue of Babylon knew nothing of. His second-choice world was just one reality in the middle of

---

[5] J. Goldingay, *Daniel*, states: 'Old Testament assumes that the results of battles on earth reflect the involvement of heaven' (p. 291).

others. Understanding his second-choice world demanded that he was able to see the huge cosmic context of what God was doing and where he was before God.

The Irish have a reputation for living in an imaginative and visionary world. It is a world of possibilities where rationalism is bent out of shape or shown to be bent itself. In the film, *Hear My Song*, Ned Beatty plays Micky O'Neil, a Liverpool nightclub owner. The film is a very Irish story interweaving love, charm, survival, vision, good luck, mayhem, charisma and the O'Neil character surviving by his wits. To prove his love for his woman Micky tries to book Josef Locke, a famous Irish singer and British tax-exile, for his struggling Liverpool nightclub. The story is fascinating, funny and fantastical as imagination and some historical reality are woven together. A series of things need to happen for O'Neil's plans to come off and you wonder how he is going to do it. Much of what he accomplishes is through his courage, quick thinking and life-force but some things happen which you just cannot explain. Everything depends on moments of unexpected breakthrough. When O'Neil goes to get water from a river there on the other side is Josef Locke, the man he has been looking for, and from nowhere a band appears just at the right time and able to play Locke's songs. Throughout the film, grace, mystery and the imagination break through and flow with reality in the same direction. It is a great film; I liked it much more than my wife did, but then I have Irish blood.

We need to place our second-choice worlds in this sort of context, seeing them as places where God is able to break through and do what he wants to do when he wants to do it. In this Daniel-type world God initiates and sets the pace, with Daniel following hard after God's thoughts and ideas. If we want to live like this our relationship with God must not be solely focused on 'doctrine' or 'truth'; it has to be focused on God as a person: a God who is relational. Relationships are not based on rationality or prepositional truth. Relationships which are lasting, focus with life-transforming power around love, forgiveness, tenderness, hope, faith and open-spaced imagination.

Daniel had to live in a world where although the present was confusing the future was clear. Thus this mysterious world was one of massive hope. Daniel gave exiles the knowledge that this second-choice world was not for ever. Not only would it come to an end, but Daniel was saying that there was a future which would surpass the one that they had in Babylon and God was working to deliver it. As Daniel headed towards his future he knew that he had been part of something bigger than himself. Daniel had actually been a part of the future. God had been at the beginning and continuation of his second-choice experience and God would be at its end.

Chapter Sixteen

Patrick and Caroline's story

I first heard Patrick and Caroline's daughter in church one morning. I could not tell whether what I heard was a gurgle of joy or a cry of pain; it was an unusual sound to me. When I looked around I saw a girl who was about twelve years old, standing, yet being held up by her father while we sang a hymn. I found this very moving; the girl swung from side to side as she made her unusual sounds. When I looked a little closer I saw that she was really enjoying singing and swinging with her Dad. I suspected then, what became clear later, that this singing, swinging, girl whom I now know as Katie was handicapped and would be in need of help all of her life.

Patrick and Caroline have four children: Katie, Lucy, James and Sarah. Lucy and James are very healthy but Katie and Sarah have been disabled from birth. This family has challenges to face. Yet one of the things that strikes me about them all is their relational health; they seem to get on well with each other, and with people outside the family unit. The fact that two members of the family are not physically and mentally whole does not hinder that impression and somehow underlines it. Spending time with them dispels some of the myths and fears surrounding wholeness and disability. In Patrick and Caroline's home the struggles are there for all to see, exposed by the para-phernalia of wheelchairs, drug regimes and sheer hard work. For other families their disability is not always so easy to detect and sometimes much more dangerous.

For Patrick and Caroline the last twenty years have meant intensely hard work with huge challenges but also years of intense joy. They have had to handle Katie and Sarah's situation in the knowledge that this is going to be a long-term and sustained effort. What has been important for them in all of this? How have they stuck with the challenges and how will they continue to handle this long-term sustained second-choice world?

Part at least of the answer is that today is not all that matters. They have a clear sense of the importance and the unimportance of time and of the way in which God can bring about transformation as time goes by. In holding on to this basic truth they are helped both by Scripture and by the fellowship and support of the Christian community. They live their lives in the light of future transformation for all their family but especially for Katie and Sarah. They look forward to a new heaven and a new earth but also to personal transformation and gain hope and strength from their conviction that eventually Katie and Sarah will have new bodies and minds. This adds to their lives a dimension which many families miss. They are able to live focusing on the endgame and not just the next five years. This sense of eventual transformation brings with it transformation in the here and now.

They also feel that the responsibility they have is in some sense even an honour. They have been given by God a charge for life which is a weight but also a privilege. In talking with them I am powerfully reminded of the many mission-aries and pastors I know whose God-given calling, although it may be difficult, brings a deep sense of joy. Patrick and

Caroline have looked at their situation and rather than frame it in destructive bitterness and resentment they have taken this second- and no-choice world as their calling from God. I find this deeply moving, especially in a world in which people avoid responsibility and seek to live lives without significance.

The Western world is besotted with trivia. We are developing anorexia of the soul and heading for lives devoid of substance. Mindless television, tabloid journalism and a continual desire for immediate gratification dominate the West. This love of things trivial leaves us weightless. When the wind turns against us we are blown away. The consequence of avoiding the calling God gives us is this kind of weightlessness. Whatever may be the problems that Patrick and Caroline face they live lives of substance. Unlike many of us they are not going to wake up in their mid-sixties and wonder if their lives mattered. The wind has blown against them and in doing so has demonstrated the substantial foundations on which their lives have been built.

They have made important choices which have maturely matched the circumstances of their world. Patrick could have developed a more intense career as an accountant but chose not to, and Caroline laid aside opportunities in the legal profession. Disability in the family can often bring about so much pressure that marriages split as the individuals run for cover from the barrage of problems; Patrick and Caroline have been able to avoid that. Courageous, realistic, God-filled choices have been their weekly menu.

We can all learn a lot from Patrick, Caroline, Lucy and James about what it means to endure in worlds of second or no choice and do it well. But maybe even more from Katie and Sarah?

PART THREE

Plunging into second choice

Chapter Seventeen

Plunging into second choice

'His heart attacked him.'
(An Indian friend describing a heart attack)

I have been staring at this blank computer screen for a long time. I have experienced so much over the last two weeks. How can I get it on this page in front of me? I have been surrounded by so much grace, love, skill, prayer and passion that I am left temporarily stunned and speechless. (My friends know that speechlessness is not usually my problem.) I keep on looking out of the window and gazing into nothingness. I guess that I am in some sort of delightful shock. I feel as if I have won the National Lottery three times over, been forced to jump off a twenty-storey building and have landed safely and held the hand of God in a way I have never done before. I was explaining how to live in a second-choice world when suddenly I entered a new one myself. During a visit to Hyderabad in India, in the middle of writing this book, I had an unexpected and unpredictable heart attack, and at the age of forty-six was baptized into another second-choice world.

My father died of heart problems when he was forty-eight. He had a damaged heart valve which in 1959 was difficult to replace; the technology and knowledge were not available to help him or us through the process of his death. I was seven when he died and ever since then people have been telling me how much I look like my dad. Over the last few years I have had to deal with occasional fears relating to him. I have asked myself many questions. If he died at forty-eight is there a possibility that I might do the same, especially if everyone feels that I am very much like him? I share his genes; do I therefore share his physical strengths and weaknesses? Do I have his heart beating away in my body and will it betray me at about the same time as his?

Although these questions have not dominated my life they have always been there, nagging away in the background. They emerge when I feel ill, notice an unusual spot on my body or feel a pain in my gut. Unlike many men in the West I have no problem in going to the doctor if I feel I need to. My response to my gene pool has always been an eagerness to get any potential problem checked and do it quickly. I have often thought that I was just a few notches away from being a hypochondriac. I regularly have breakfast with a friend who is very similar to me, both of us being imaginative extroverts. The difference between Peter and myself is that he often *thinks* he is sick while I *know* I am. It's wonderful to have a lively imagination, but now and again it can work against you; imagination is a blade which cuts both ways.

I went to India in January 1999 to look at a very exciting leadership programme which had been developed for people heading for senior leadership in church and para-church organizations. On the morning of my third day there I did not feel too well but was not greatly concerned. When I was living in India in 1977 I had an emergency operation to take out my appendix. I thought that this sort of experience was not going to be repeated; I was shockingly wrong.

It was nine o'clock in the morning, and I was speaking to a small group of trainers and administrators when I began to feel a pain in the left side and at the centre of my chest. I had felt this pain before over the previous two months when I had exerted myself in running or walking but I put it down to some sort of chest infection which would soon clear up. While I was speaking I felt that I wanted to get out of the room and realized my usual power in delivery had deserted me. After I had finished I only wanted to go outside and sit down. I was feeling nauseous and quite weak. By now I was sure I had some new form of jet lag or had eaten something which did not agree with me. I sat outside for a few moments watching some young boys playing cricket. They wanted to impress me but I was not to be impressed. I could only feel my chest and the monkey-grip pain which it contained.

After meeting with a friend I excused myself, saying I wanted to go to my room and rest. He graciously asked if I needed any help but I refused. I lay down for about ten minutes but the pain did not subside; instead a new pain began in my arm. Since neither jet lag nor eating the wrong thing gives you a pain in the arm I decided it was time to get help. I walked downstairs and told someone working there in the building that I had a pain in my chest — could he get help? I walked back upstairs and lay down. Within a couple of minutes two friends came into the room. Both looked extremely concerned. I have known Marcus and Alfy for over twenty years and I knew Alfy was an expert on hearts. He had had by-pass surgery eleven years before and was famed for advice on hearts and health. He looked at me with deep worry on his face and said, 'Viv, you are having what I had' — then raced off to get a vehicle to take me to hospital. I thought Alfy was wrong but I was ready to go if he thought it important.

In the back of the van I bounced through the town of Hyderabad while Alfy decided which hospital to go to. Alfy and Marcus prayed for me and gave me a pill which seemed to melt away from under my tongue. I lay there feeling the pain but also feeling embarrassed; this was not my idea of the dramatic all-consuming chest ripper I imagined a heart attack to be. I felt sure I was going to arrive at the hospital and have some tests, after which the doctor would advise me to take a day's rest and everything would be fine. I was wrong, very wrong.

At the hospital I was wheeled through doors marked CARDIOLOGY into what appeared to be a long corridor. Then all hell — or was it heaven? — seemed to break loose. India was moving fast, very fast, and I was at the centre of the whirlwind. I was lowered on to a bed and then found myself surrounded by people doing all sorts of things to me. One put something in my mouth; another started sticking things on my chest while Alfy and Marcus stood to the side. Then I heard a voice of authority. An Indian stood beside my bed and announced his name and qualifications, then explained the situation to me with exceptional and shocking clarity. 'You are having a heart attack right now!' said Dr Viswenath. He offered me a choice: I could receive drug therapy which might or might not work or he could do some procedure (he got technical on me at that point), which would work. I was sick but not stupid; I decided to go for the latter. (All the seminars I have led on decision-making clearly helped.)

That was the moment that I was plunged into my second-choice world. I knew my life was hanging in a place where I did not want it to hang, and that I might not get out of that hospital alive, see my wife again or ever regain my health. It was as though I had walked to the top of the very tall building and some unseen hand had pushed me off. I was falling and falling with no idea whether I was going to crash onto the concrete below or whether I was going to descend in a smooth curve like some Disneyland ride.

People were still racing around the ward, the authoritative doctor was still shouting at his nurses, and everyone looked anxious and serious. But as I lay on my intensive-care bed I had entered into my own world, a world where no one could come but me. Maybe when you are pushed off the top of a building the first thing you feel is aloneness . . . that no one is with you . . . there is no community alongside . . . the fall is all yours. Maybe you feel the aloneness before you feel the fear? Splayed out on my bed I thought of Jesus on his cross. He had been fundamentally and absolutely alone, forsaken by his friends and even by his Father. I was hanging on my bed and he was hanging on his cross; both of us were alone.

My mind began to shoot off in a thousand directions. Captain Kirk had ordered some warp factor and my mind was streaking through space. Fear gripped stronger than the pain in my chest. The doctor had told me that he was going to do something which worked but I had no idea what it was. In my imagination I was sure he would be giving me a powerful sedative after which he would dig into my chest to remove the blockage from my heart. I visualized a gardener digging down to find a weed in the grass and ripping it out by the roots. I did not want to be awake for that, but neither did I want to go to sleep in case it was for the last time.

The shock and fear were two terrible twins. The instant slip from feeling that I would be fine in a couple of hours to realizing that I could be dead very soon induced a sudden rush of profound insecurity and powerlessness. The fear I felt at that moment was unlike any I had experienced before.

In 1977 I had a 'face-off' with a monkey on the roof of a Kathmandu hotel. I thought the space on the roof was mine and the monkey did not agree. Confidently I tried to chase it away but the monkey would not move. He turned his head, swung his body around and ran at me, demonstrating that the space was his! This fear on the bed in Hyderabad was like the another encounter with an Asian monkey. My fear was urgent and vibrant, as if some vicious monkey had leaped on to my chest and from there sought to dominate all it surveyed. Meanwhile I was reaching depths of fear which I had never known; the fear was all around me; I was saturated in it.

Then, but I don't know quite when because time was strangely meaningless, something or someone entered the scene. I saw no angel or vision of Jesus but fear was no longer the centre. The monkey was no longer gripping my chest; he was on his way to stand by the wall.

Three weeks later, when I got home, my colleagues gave me a huge card with a picture of a duckling tucked safely inside somebody's pocket. When I saw it the image resonated with these moments when I, like the duckling, was enfolded by a sense of rightness and was scooped up by assurance. I am not sure how the medication affected me and I am struggling for words but I want to call this moment an entry of grace. I had a sense of the arrival of God. This did not mean that I was going to live, or that everything would be fine, but that all of this was somehow right. The fear had not totally left me but it had gone to the right place. My life did not pass before me, as is supposed to happen if you drown, but I was very much aware of the whole of my life as it had been lived up to then, during those fully lived yet potentially deathly moments.

In my aloneness I felt what I can only describe as a sense of celebration and completeness. Maybe the word celebration gives the idea of bands playing and partying crowds, but I don't know another word to use. I was somehow living with the smile and approval of God. Not because I had lived a great life or because I was special but because there was no sense of regret. Somehow I was aware that although my life had been far from perfect and was flawed in many of its dimensions, that did not matter. God was there and telling me that I had lived well. This was not a time of regret or rebuke but celebration: a sense that in spite of the fear and the falling, things were going well.

In the middle of the paradox of falling, fear and celebrating grace was my wife Sheila. She was in London, thousands of miles and many hours away. What would she do if I died? And so I became very practical. It seemed crazy that she was in London and was not here with me going through this crisis. I kept on thinking that we should move to Canada as fast as possible and I became frustrated with myself for not having insisted on that a couple of years ago. Sheila is Canadian and all of her family are in British Columbia or Washington State. I found myself wondering what she would do if I did not get out of this intensive-care unit. Maybe I had just entered my last building and had had my last journey on a road? If this surgeon was to go digging in my heart it might not work? I might die before he had time to get there? What about blood transfusions? What about HIV and hepatitis B and all the other dangers of invasive procedures? If my betraying heart was rescued from its wandering I might be killed by these other dangers. Oh God! Oh Sheila!

Through all these jangling thoughts the authoritative doctor was asking me questions. Did I smoke? Did I feel nausea? What other operations had I had? Then a string of other questions which seemed meaningless to me but clearly mattered to him. People still seemed to be moving very fast when I was handed a form and a pen. I signed whatever it was and the doctor passed it to Alfy for him to sign as well. Then a man started shaving my body from mid-chest to mid-thigh. I wondered why he was doing that if they were going to go digging into my heart? What had my thigh got to do with this?

They lifted me on to a trolley and started to wheel me away. Then another wave of fear hit me. I thought I was heading for a general anaesthetic and who knows where after that. I called out to Alfy, 'If I die, tell Sheila I love her.' This appeared to get me in trouble. Alfy seemed to shout , 'Viv, you are not going to die,' then my doctor seemed upset with me as he too seemed to shout, 'You are not going to die.' I remember feeling that he was the last man I wanted to upset right now. I also remember praying that he was not an anti-Christian, Hindu radical who might imagine he could be serving his gods by getting rid of me. (India was going through a period of anti-Christian persecution led by Hindu extremists and this was feeding into my imagination.)

I was wheeled down the corridor and into the lift for my journey to the operating theatre. What concerned me most were the faces surrounding me. Their expressions seemed to reflect the trouble I was in. Those faces were sapping my optimism, telling me I was going to die regardless of what Alfy or my doctor said. I can remember trying to make a joke in the lift but I was the only one who laughed. Was my sense of humour being damaged along with my heart?

In the operating theatre I was greeted by eight or nine people dressed in green. There was an air of competence and confidence about this team; gone were the worried-looking people in the lift, I was in a new world. There was an impressive display of technology and a down-draught from the air conditioning; I was very cold and started to shake. I now know that this was the turning point. If I was falling off the Dorchester Hotel then this was the moment when I began my curve upwards out of the vertical descent.

Instead of administering the knockout drug I was anticipating, the doctor told me he was going to work on my leg. My leg? Again I wondered . . . whatever had my leg to do with my heart attack? He explained that this was the route he was going to take to my heart and I remembered that my mother had always told me that the way to a man's heart was through his stomach. I was conscious throughout the whole procedure. The doctor spent most of his time looking at a video screen and talking as he carried out what I now know was an angioplasty. He was inserting a balloon and placing a mesh into an artery of my heart to sort out the blockage and support the artery. I was free of pain and very happy that he was not gardening into my chest to find the weeds. After what seemed like twenty minutes he looked at me and told me that I had had a 100 per cent blockage but the procedure had been 100 per cent successful. He then said to me, 'Do you want to see what I have done?' Absolutely! He turned the video screen towards me and explained that everything he had done was recorded on CD ROM, so I lay back and watched the show. I saw my heart as it was before the intervention, the new blood flow afterwards, and a close-up of the mesh left inside. He told me that it was unlikely that many hospitals in England would have such modern facilities and I discovered later that he was right.

Within a couple of hours and back in intensive care my doctor came to see me and said, 'You are a very lucky bastard! — please excuse my French.' He explained that if I had not received the care I needed when I did that I would have lost 80 per cent of my heart function but as it is I had probably lost 10 to 20 per cent. He explained that my heart would grow to compensate for the loss I had sustained and that I could look forward to a normal healthy life. He told me that I had other heart problems which needed to be sorted out. One of them was important but not urgent and I might need some other procedure in the future. What had begun as a push off a tall building and the free fall which followed was now in reverse. I was now rising in elation. I had survived. I was going to live and live well. My doctor was wrong about one thing. My heart damage was much less than he imagined.

It was a wonderful moment when Sheila and my colleague Rosemary Morris walked into my room at the hospital a couple of days later. Due to excellence, love and thoughtfulness from so many friends and colleagues in England and India they arrived in Hyderabad. We cried, laughed and breathed sighs of relief. Underneath it all was recognition that life is a gift from God.

These two women were and still are amazing! In the middle of all I had been through I was wondering how Sheila would take this trauma. Sheila had heard the news from my colleague Joseph just as she was about to get up and go to work. How can you tell anyone that 'your husband is fine but he has just had a heart attack'? Joseph had that job, at which point Sheila was plunged, along with me, into this second- and no-choice world and a horrendous journey from London to India. Sheila has her own story to tell regarding all this but by the time she arrived in Hyderabad we were both as taut and tense as an elastic band.

It was when everyone left the hospital room and Sheila and I were alone that my feelings burst through; my chest did not heave with pain but with tears. I don't think I have ever cried like that in my life. The tears were for the joy at being alive, holding my wife in my arms and the euphoric relief that I had come very close to death and yet it had passed me by. Woven into my joy and relief was the knowledge that a twenty-one-year-old had died in the hospital in the bed next to me during my first night in intensive care. Somehow, I had survived and he had not.

Who in the West would have thought that Hyderabad, India, would be a wonderful place to have a heart attack? Whom would I have rather had next to me in the initial crisis of a heart attack than the by-pass-experienced Alfy Franks? Who would have thought that I would have a skilled cardiologist so quickly available with all the equipment needed? Who would have thought that after three weeks I would be back in England typing these words and surrounded by cards, phone calls, visits, family and friends telling me over and over again that they love me and that I must not do that again?

On my flight out of Hyderabad to London, while I was waiting in the transit lounge, I started talking to a businessman. I asked him what he did and where he was going. He was from England, on his way to Shanghai and he was hating the journey. He asked me what I was doing. I said, 'I came here to have my heart attack.' He headed off to Shanghai confused. But to me the whole experience was as bright as a sun-filled dawn.

PART FOUR

Angles at work in second choice

Chapter Eighteen

Love and second choice

*If I have faith that can remove mountains, but
have not love, I am nothing.* (1 Corinthians 13:2)

Then he lay down close by and whispered with
a smile, 'I love you right up to the moon — and
back.'
(Big Nutbrown Hare to Little Nutbrown Hare in
Sam McBratney: *Guess How Much I love You*[1])

Many of us get into our second-choice worlds because of
love, or rather because we are in love. Although we may
want to avoid a certain set of circumstances love draws us
into them and demands that we live with them. One of
love's characteristics is that it constantly draws us away
from many of our initial and sometimes instinctive first
choices and calls us to second or no choice. One of the
chief problems of the Western world today is that our
fixation with living in our first-choice worlds reflects our
inability to love or our failure to understand love's true
nature. The idea that 'good' means that which is good for
me is so deeply engrained in modern society that we

---

[1] 1994, Walker Books.

barely notice it. Because we are so deluded and confused by our own self-love we cannot conceive of any love of which we are not the centre. This confronts us with an immense danger and also a challenge: if we do not recover the sort of love which will enable us to live with second choice we are doomed to a sterile relationship primarily with ourselves. When old age comes we will be condemned to replaying in our minds endless home movies — starring ourselves.

In December 1998 popular music in Britain was dominated by one song. Sung by Cher, it included a repetitive, dominant and echoing line, 'Do you believe in life after love?' The song seemed to be asking the questions we ask ourselves after a romance is over, and the underlying message seemed to be: 'I think I will survive but I'm not sure about you, my ex-love.' It is one of those songs which stuck in my mind like flypaper — as I am sure was the producer's intention — but it seemed to be asking some good questions. It was only when I watched the MTV video version of the song that I realized the sheer outrageous triviality of the song. The story played out in the video takes place in one evening. A girl goes to a party and sees a boy; they are mutually attracted and appear to fall in 'love' with each other. The video ends with her realizing that he has another girl. While he walks home with her Cher watches them from the roof. Throughout the whole process Cher is the singing mentor-mother figure asking her repetitive question about whether there is life after love. The song and video combined seem to answer the question — What is love? — by saying that it is a series of feelings and attractions which can emerge and subside in a couple of hours at a party. The appalling thing about the song is its overwhelming triviality. Yet if this is not love — then what is it?

Love means being able to embrace a world of second choice. It has the ability to displace the agenda of self and first choice and reach out towards the other while possessing the potential of being able to live with what you do not really want. Paul was able to explain the nature of love with considerably more insistence than Cher in her 'Believe' song.

Writing to a lively but confused church in Corinth, Paul uses radical language in 1 Corinthians 13 in order to express the nature of love in a series of contrasts. Without love our lives are empty — like 'resounding gongs or clanging cymbals'. In other words without love our lives are all noise and surface but empty. Without love, says Paul, our emptiness is matched only by our nothingness. We can have 'the gift of prophecy and can fathom all mysteries and all knowledge' and yet be — nothing. Paul is addressing people who are aware of their gifts and talents; he warns them that significance does not come out of how well we do what we do. That is not what truly makes us persons. Whatever our gifts, we are reduced to nothingness unless we are able to live relationally: unless we are able to love and be loved.

Having shown what love is not, Paul goes on to describe how we can recognize it when we see it. Love is patient, love is kind, love gives people ample time and tenderness. Love hangs around and waits for people to recover from sickness, children to learn to read, old people to express their ideas. Love goes from season to season, waiting if necessary. Because love is not very 'efficient' or fast it challenges the values of the contemporary Western world. Our lack of love is often evidenced in our inability to hang around and wait, our inability to let others be first.

It seems to me that Paul is teaching us that without love we are like ships at sea, pitching and rolling powerlessly in the night. Love acts like ballast. It brings us back into equilibrium because it fills our lives with substance. The less we love the more danger we are in. The more we love and are loved the greater the chance of avoiding catastrophe.

The paradox of love

This is where the transformation takes place and we enter a world of paradox. For when our love propels us into a second-choice world it becomes first choice even though there may be many things about it which we would want to change. Love is an overarching sanity which enters into a mad second-choice world and works. We find ourselves in the paradox of doing things we really do not want to do because we really want to do them. We go through this split world because we love.

Why was it that in 1991 a friend of mine should decide to take her expensively acquired Canadian nursing skills and face deprivation, mud, sickness and pressure in order to donate her gifts to the Kurds who had fled into the mountains to escape from Sadam Hussein? Why is it that another friend who earns a lot of money in his successful business gives much of it away to help finance programmes for the poor in countries which are not his own? Why is it that another friend of mine has held on to a marriage over two decades even though his partner is not able to return his love in a way which is recognizable? Are these people obsessed? Are they sick? Stupid? Are they driven by some sort of need for self-punishment? It is possible to live out this sort of sacrifice for many reasons, yet I am sure the possibilities I have listed are not their primary drives. I think the real reason behind their motivation is that they love: they are love-driven. There may well be other issues which motivate them but the backbone and core of their actions and aspirations is love. They have chosen to give their lives and resources to causes of which they are not the centre and which do not benefit them chiefly. Second-choice situations become first choice when we love and the glorious paradox of the good news of Jesus, the source of love. is established once again — in our lives.

Love does not make those choices easy but it does make them real. There is something about people who love and head for second choice which is authentic and clear. When love leads us into second choice we have to lay aside images and perceptions of ourselves but in the process a new and real image emerges. I know people who live this way and they possess something quite remarkable: a sort of beauty intermingled with strength which is so attractive that others want to spend time with them and have them for friends. Models on the catwalks or film stars are pale emaciated shadows compared to these second-choice people.

Once we grasp this basic truth we realize that our images of success have to be transformed. This transformation is well overdue in the Western world.

So the truth is that love leads us into second-choice worlds. Yet when we think realistically — and biblically — about this, we would not really have it any other way. We shall not be destabilized by the insecurity or tempted by the desire for approval that leads some people to transform their faces through unnecessary plastic surgery and others to build muscle through steroid abuse. When offered the imperfect, love says 'Fine' and accepts the problems with open eyes and a willing heart.

Chapter Nineteen

Integrated living

Scott Fitzgerald once said that the test of a
first-class mind was the ability to hold two
opposing ideas in the head at the same time
and still retain the ability to function.
(Charles Handy, *The Empty Raincoat*[1])

God's people were called to live in Babylon in a context
dominated by superstition, omens and fear. Daniel and his
Hebrew friends responded to this by embracing Babylon
in every way possible, consistent with their responsibility
to God. They chose to live their faith and yet be integrated
into the heavily contaminated world of Babylon. So, in the
embrace of their second-choice world they affirmed that it
was not Nebuchadnezzar, Belshazzar or Darius who was
in control . . . but God.

Daniel was a victim of huge waves of military might and
court intrigue. He lived in the situation given to him with
full vigour, regardless of the hopes, possibilities and dreams
which related to the end of the exile that he and his people
were suffering. Daniel discovered that the important point

---

[1] C. Handy, p. 18.

was not being concerned about the removal of the mess of Babylon but submitting to it. He lived there and it was home. Daniel chose to live in the continual now of his second-choice world and not some distant dream of what should be.

The lifelong grind of second-choice worlds demands lifelong strategies for coping with their reality. This means that whichever way the wind blows we have to recognize and respond to it. To pretend that our second-choice world is our first choice usually leads to disaster. Denying that we are in a second- or no-choice world may have some appeal; but all it does is intensify the pain when we finally admit that things are not going well for us.

This perspective also applied to Daniel's gifting. He was exceptionally gifted and had to live what he was and not just where he was. It was his gifting which projected him to the centre of his second-choice world. If God had not made Daniel so gifted then he would not have had to face most of the trials and tribulations of his second-choice world. Without his gifts of intelligence, vision and courage he could have had a reasonable and quiet life. Sometimes, the very gifts we pray for are the things which will send us into worlds of second choice.

This question of gifting is posed very powerfully in the film *Good Will Hunting*. Although Will is a maths genius he works as a cleaner at a prestigious college. While he cleans the lecture rooms, he solves near impossible maths problems left by professors for their classes. Will's friend is concerned about this and expresses his frustration in a pivotal scene: Will is living below his potential, he is not living with what has been given to him, he should not be a cleaner or work on a building site, he should be making a contribution in maths, the area of his gifting. The friend expects that one day when he comes to collect Will for work he will be gone. In fact Will's friend hopes he will have disappeared and gone to work in an environment more related to his gifting This would be inspirational to his friend. There is, however, a reason for Will's choice. He is an angry and broken young man who has not learned how to love others or accept himself. Will was on the run from himself living a split life without integration. The film is saying that we do not live well if we deny what we are and seek to be something else.

The question for Will is the question for us all. Are we able to integrate all the aspects of our lives and make them whole? Can Will face his history, his internal brokenness and his inability to love? Can we?

Central to Daniel's ability to live with his givenness was his ability to live with complexity. Daniel had to live with his personal history and the purposes of God for his nation. This was linked with an anticipation of the future and all of what God was going to do. In the middle of this, Daniel's focus had to be on living in Babylon, and nowhere else. It was Daniel's interaction with these aspects of his givenness which enabled him to understand and accept his life in Babylon.

We are prevented from living well in the space between our first- and second-choice worlds because, for whatever reason, we fail to integrate all of what we are into the reality of our lives. We choose to live with a split and shattered self and hope that somehow neither we nor others will notice. We hide from ourselves and do all we can to avoid one part of our lives fully encountering the other. Living well in a second-choice world requires us to have a whole and integrated conversation with ourselves.

We have to bring the strands of our lives together, making a complete yet ragged whole. Why do we find it so hard to achieve this? The primary reason is shame. Our sense of guilt and failure so overwhelms us that although we hide through a succession of projected images, we want people to see what we do rather than what we are. We want people to be focused on what we wear rather than deal with what we are like inside. Yet, the truth seeps through. We want people to believe that we are powerful, wealthy and in control, but after knowing us for a while they are able to see that our image does not reflect anything of value. Often we are tempted to take the easy way out — don't make any friends. The tragedy is that in cutting ourselves off from friends we are also cutting ourselves off from grace.

Uli was in her late seventies. She had been a Christian since her late teens and had lived a life of devotion to God, doing all the things that Christians in her culture are intended to do and avoiding all the things they should avoid. She was bright, loved Christian doctrine and enjoyed arguing theology. Yet throughout her life Uli was driven by shame. She was never able to really face the pain of her childhood in rural Germany and all of the shame which she lived through. Even knowing Christian doctrine and holding well-argued and strong theological positions did not help her. Her shame and the attendant denial were so strong that she slipped into a life of hypocrisy. She talked one way but lived another, building inner and outer walls so effectively that she could not understand the construction of herself. One result was that others could not climb the walls so as to talk to the 'real' hidden Uli.

This was Uli's tragedy. She was a Christian all of her life but the gospel was not able to do in and for her what it might have done. The gospel is all about integration. Holiness and shame meet each other in Jesus and the latter is dealt with. Secure in our relationship with a loving and accepting God we can face ourselves, embrace the shame and experience the arrival of profound joy. This is how a God of grace works in human lives. On the cross Jesus accepted the shame, took the curse — and died. Yet he rose again from the dead and in doing so he proclaimed victory over the tragedies of personal history and shame. Now he reassures and invites us, telling us that there is a life to be lived: an integrated life where our personal horror meets his grace and where we shall discover ourselves for the first time.

Chapter Twenty

Embrace the chaos

> The West has exhausted its inner possibilities.
> (Carver Yu: *Being Relational*[1])

The West has been steeped in rationalism over the last two hundred years, dominated by logic, scepticism and science. The underlying assumption, both insistent and seductive, has been that the world is a rational place and that if we could just understand it then we could master it. If we could tame the dark forces of nature and sickness we would be able to take control of our environment and set the agenda for ourselves and our world. Yet today the whole agenda is being questioned and rejected, as Carver Yu has pointed out:

> One of the phenomena which immediately strikes us as a possible sign of a cultural dilemma is the gulf between technological optimism and literary pessimism in the West. Amidst great scientific achievements of which man should be proud, we hear some of the most passionate indictments against man by literary artists.[2]

---

[1] C. Yu, 1987, p. 6.
[2] C. Yu, 1987, p. 1.

We have accomplished wonders on one side yet we see people falling apart on the other and it is our writers and poets, Christian and non-Christian, who let us know this is so.

The Hebrew community in Babylon had minimal control over their circumstances. In a very real sense their world had fallen apart. There was no big decision that they could take in order to be freed from bondage, no surge of strength which would have liberated them. Daniel and his friends had to flex with the chaos and become integrated with it. There was no rational linear world for them. What they experienced was continual turbulence throughout the Babylonian experience.

Living a God-centred life means submitting our own agenda to his. As I lay in intensive care in Hyderabad knowing that my heart was giving way within me I could feel the control of my life slipping away. My own personal chaos was wrapped into body and spirit. But there were much greater forces at work than I and the only option open to me as I lay there was to surf through the chaos of it all. This kind of experience is not so uncommon; we can go through whole decades believing that we are living logical and rational lives which we control, but all it needs is one heart attack, losing a job or seeing our partner walking out on us — and our perspective is changed. This loss of control does not mean failure or even weakness. For Daniel and his fellow Hebrews it was just the arena in which they had to work and to which they had to adapt.

One important difference between being a Hebrew and being a Babylonian was that the Hebrews knew they were in trouble and the Babylonians did not; the Babylonians believed that their destiny was in their own hands. With startling similarity to today's modern world the Babylonians were in fantasy about how far and for how long they could control their world. They not only perceived themselves as being in control — they clung to this fantasy right up to the time when everything shifted beneath them and they realized at last that this was not so.

Living realistically demands that we anticipate and even embrace the chaos of the world in which we live. Even if our lives look good and we are feeling fine there are many people in our communities who are not. The fact that our towns are impressive, our roads are clean and we have a telephone system which works can make us believe that all is well. But the reality is otherwise. Inside those towns, on those roads and talking on the telephones are people burdened — with anxieties, sins, complexes and aspirations. They are mixtures of rational and irrational; joy and misery; hope and despair; living with their past and anticipating some sort of future.

The book of Acts explains what life was like for the early church. These first Christians did not live in a controlled and rational environment; they had to live and work with chaos. Although they believed that God was in charge of it all, most of the time they had to take that on trust and wait to see how things went. Embracing chaos is the essence of living a faith-filled exciting life, the kind of life in which we are able to see God do things which we could never imagine. When we are living this kind of life we are fully alive.

As I watched *The Truman Show* I experienced one or two chilling moments. In this film Jim Carey lived in a pretend and commercially driven world where everything worked well. The sun rose on time; the rain came regularly and his wife was perfect. Yet there was something wrong with his perfect world: he was not really alive. Discovering this was devastating. For me the chilling moments came as I realized how the film related to the way Christians perceive their world. Carey's world of perfection is the sort of world that I think many Christians want — and non-Christians too. A 'nice' world with no problems: a world where being problem-free demonstrates how closely you are walking with God. The film successfully rips that world apart and insists that however long you live in your own construction of niceness, the whole lot will eventually come falling down around your ears. Jim Carey's world and the real world of the book of Acts are utterly opposed to each other. In that real world — and today — Christians do die, face judgement, get shipwrecked, have their worlds turned upside down, disagree with each other and suffer persecution. Yet for all of its chaos and pain this world is real. Most importantly, it is a world where the gospel is able to bring salt, light and healing to an even more chaotic world.

Chapter Twenty-one

Live a mentored life

The greatest errors in the spiritual life are
not committed by the adepts. The greatest
capacity for self-deceit in prayer comes not in
the early years but in the middle and late years.
(Eugene Peterson: *Working the Angles*[1])

I have come to the conclusion that I am one of the richest
men I know. I am so rich that it is overwhelming, exciting
and a bigger responsibility than I thought.

The hurricane that followed the heart attack

In recent weeks I have not just been hit by a heart attack. I
have also been in the middle of a glorious hurricane. The
hurricane force of my family, community, church and friends
has surrounded me. I have had more affirmation, attention,
offers of help, declarations of love, anger at the thought of
my loss, tears on my behalf, cards, e-mails, phone calls and
prayers than I can just stand. Is this what it means to be

---

[1] E. Peterson, p. 41.

wealthy? I am sinking under a weight of love yet at the same time it is buoying me up.

When I meet people they really mean with all their hearts that they are 'glad to see' me. Now, when people ask, 'How are you?' I have to answer with clarity, truthfulness and adequate reflection because what people are communicating is that they really want to know. They won't be satisfied with 'Fine, thanks', or a quick response of 'How are *you*?' These days our conversations are so often interspersed with meaningful silences and at present it is as though there is a sense of awe around the whole story of my being alive and none of us knows how to react. I hope it is that and not the drugs I am taking! This relational heat may cool down in a couple of months but for now it is intense and wonderful.

Where has this hurricane come from? Do other people get this sort of attention when they have been close to death? What about all those people who never see anyone from one week to the next? Do the many people who live alone get this sort of attention? Why am I so overwhelmed by love that I often feel like crying — yet others are so fundamentally alone?

I think this kind of difference is often rooted in the nature of the choices we make before we tumble into the world of second choice. I am reaping a hundredfold the investment I have made in people over the last thirty years. I feel it's not been a massive investment but the tiny contribution which I have made to quite a large number of people is now coming back to me. The small breeze of love which I sent out is returning like some intense weather system, powerful enough to knock me off my feet. To go through second-choice worlds and flourish we need friends, good friends on whom we can lean and from whom we can learn, people who can knock us off our feet with their commitment, love and wisdom. As I read about Daniel, it seems to me that the Hebrews in Babylon had that sort of community.

The larger context

Individualism and self were not the centre of the Hebrews' experience in their second-choice Babylonian world. Daniel and his friends were part of something larger than their own aspirations of personal fulfilment and their own self-actualization. They lived out their individuality in the context of community and friends. They were also in a wider relationship which included their fellow exiles, the Babylonians, and God. This larger context enabled them to place self in its proper perspective and opened the door to effective and rich encounter with the Babylonian culture.

This network of relationships is immensely important. One kind of supportive relationship that has attracted attention recently in the secular as well as the religious world is 'mentoring'. A mentor, according to the Shorter Oxford Dictionary, is 'an experienced and trusted adviser or guide; a teacher, a tutor'.

If you are to flourish in second-choice worlds you need a friend or friends to walk with you in the process. Kenneth Leech calls a person who does this a 'Soul Friend'. Leech begins his book on the subject by quoting a Celtic saying: 'Anyone without a friend is a body without a head.' Leech suggests that your Soul Friend should be a person who is possessed by the Spirit, one who has experience, learning and discernment — a person who gives way to the Holy Spirit. It would be wonderful to have friends with such qualifications but many of us do not have this sort of person available to us. Eugene Peterson suggests that 'spiritual direction takes place when two people agree to give their full attention to what God is doing in one (or both) of their lives and seek to respond in faith'. When we allow someone into our inner world and trust them with our own story helpful revelation can be the result.

One of the great challenges of our age is seeing if we can hold on to and develop mentoring relationships. Can we see a growing movement of healthy spiritual direction, biblical discipleship, good examples and people showing other people the way forward with their lives? Clergy and church leaders have abandoned their calling in droves but have kept their jobs and titles, having 'metamorphosed into a company of shopkeepers, and the shops they keep are churches'.[2] What chance is there for those who follow to do any better?

We have to resist modern lies, for example, that self is the centre of life and that a worthwhile existence is to be defined as how well we live our lives. The only way to do this adequately is through living a mentored life — a life in community where others are able to warn, influence and love us in a way which will cause us to mature into what God intended us to be. It may well be that our friends and mentors have no idea of what precisely that is but they will be able help in the process.

I have just spent two hours with Steve. He is typical of many middle-aged men in the West. He has done very well at his job in the City of London and has made enough money to be comfortable for the rest of his life. Steve is a man who suffers from a deep sense of betrayal. He feels that he has lived life with a focus on fulfilling goals, getting results and controlling his world. He has lived much of his

---

[2] Peterson, p. 2. Peterson's introduction to the book is both surgical and compassionate: a rare combination.

life in classic Western evangelical style, free of mentoring. Now in his early forties, he has just discovered that he has very few friends. There are many people with whom he can share ideas but no one who will help him access himself, walk with him through times of stress and help him keep God-focused. If Steve is to move forward he is going to need good friends who will teach him how to feel as well as think. The job is likely to take a long time.

The sort of friend Steve needs is the sort of friend I had in Forrest. Forrest and I both attended Regent College in Vancouver in the middle of the nineties. After chatting a little about our lives and doing a college course together Forrest and I decided to be Soul Friends to each other. We met once a week over lunch with the idea of reflecting through each other's lives and expressing how we felt. We decided to start with an explanation of how we were getting along with God. I went first, meandering through how I thought things were going, thinking I had explained myself very well. I sat back waiting for Forrest's approval and affirmation. It did not come in the way I anticipated. Forrest said, 'Viv, it seems to me that you have a relationship with an idea rather than with God.' I was a little stunned by this so I asked him if I could say a bit more. Being a professional explainer, as a preacher and teacher, I wanted to be sure that Forrest was listening properly. I said my second piece and waited for more developed feedback. Forrest continued, 'Viv, it still sounds like you have a relationship with some great ideas rather than a personal God.' I could feel myself sinking inside. We had lunch, prayed a little together and I was off to do my work.

The next two days were fascinating and worth their weight in diamonds to me. I thought I knew exactly what Forrest was saying. I had drifted into being a professional explainer of the Bible; my head was full of wonderful truths and principles but there was a fog in the middle of the explanation of these truths. In seeking to be clear in communication of the things about God I was missing out on a relationship with him. My life was gathering around truth rather than the One who is truth. What happened over that simple lunchtime meeting still shapes me. What I learned from Forrest was so fundamental that I doubt I will ever forget it. I knew the truth of what he was saying before we talked, but only in a general way. I could tell anyone that they needed to pay attention to their relationship with God rather than to truth about him. But it took a relationship with a clear-thinking and spiritual friend to point out how this was working out in me.

Soul Friends, spiritual directors, mentors and good company all help us to listen well. In second-choice worlds the quality of our listening is pivotal if we are going to be able to flourish. Being attentive to what God is saying to us through our stresses and pressures can have a powerful influence on whether the second-choice world we are in will remain a desert or be amazingly transformed into a garden.

What gets in the way of living a mentored life? Usually it is a mixture of ignorance, laziness and pride. We just don't know how important it is, we know but cannot be bothered, or we know but just cannot face someone else understanding the deceptions of our own hearts. To transform the nature of a second- or no-choice world we have to face these sins head-on.

Chapter Twenty-two

Being subversive

> Later he saw Jesus move from tree to tree in the
> back of his mind, a wild ragged figure motioning
> to him to turn around and come off into the dark
> where he was not sure of his footing.
> (Flannery O'Connor: *Wise Blood*[1])

Why were the Hebrews so influential in Babylon? Primarily
because of the way they lived their day-to-day lives. It was
the faithful way they used their basic gifting which eventually opened up the significant leaders in the culture to
the God of Daniel and the Hebrews. It was faithful endurance which was pivotal in cutting into this culture; prophetic
passion and vision followed later.

Daniel lived an integrated life, not only in the way he
embraced his complex personal life but also in the way he
interacted with the culture of Babylon. His relationship with
God was expressed in the way he engaged with his tasks.
All of his spirituality was lived through what he did, which
was in turn woven into all that he was. Daniel succeeded
in integrating an intensive political life with a healthy

---

[1] p. 13.

relationship with God. When he was given authority and power he exercised both without fracturing his internal world. There is an integration of all that he was: an intellectual, an administrator, a visionary, a leader and a dreamer, but all were integrated and brought together in a single pattern of living. In this way Daniel was able to live subversively.

Christian subversion

What does this mean? It means that Daniel was able to see the transformation of situations and individuals around him in a way which was both subtle and, in its implications and consequences, revolutionary. Without declaring open war on the Babylonian culture and values Daniel and his Hebrew friends were able to participate in huge shifts regarding how Babylon responded to their God.

Second-choice worlds are places for subversion. We have to try and work though the implications of living where we don't want to, doing it well and go further to actually influence our world. This is one of the realities which will eventually undo the cult of first being everything. History shows how powerful this approach can be. When I was in Iran in 1976 the picture of the Shah seemed to be in every house and on every shop wall. The people of Iran appeared proud of him but what seemed to be obvious was not the case. We now know that while the picture of the Shah was hung on many walls, very different versions were being displayed in people's minds. From Paris, Muslim fundamentalism was running a huge subversion programme which included the distribution of thousands of cassette tapes preparing people for the coming revolution. It was not long before pictures of the mullahs and Khomeini replaced the pictures of the Shah in particular.

It is as people watch us go though our second-choice world and do it well that the subversion takes place. How we cope with disappointment, how we respond to suffering, how we react to losing dignity and how we cope with authority — all speak with compelling eloquence to a needy world. We live in a world where people do not trust the media, which constantly bombards them with messages which seek to separate them from their money, a world which continually puts pressure on people to change their allegiance or value systems. The crying need is for authenticity. Second-choice worlds open up the opportunity for seeing that authenticity demonstrated.

The declaration of the kingdom and good news of God needs to be clear. But speaking it is not enough. People in the West are increasingly sceptical of promotional programmes of any sort. Advertising, tele-evangelists and general hype mean that we must learn how to live subversively. Jesus did this all the time. He often spoke obliquely, avoided the obvious, did not answer direct questions and would not follow the agenda that others tried to impose on him. Yet many people were drawn to him, listened to his words and were attracted by his life.

A long haul

It is often when people around us enter into their second- or no-choice world that they remember how we coped with ours. As they recall what we did and how we did it, our remembered behaviour becomes a source of light in the darkness they are experiencing. People who live well in their second-choice worlds need to have patience to see what God will do through them over the long haul. Occasionally the 'long haul' may extend even beyond our own death. The important thing is that we have lived lives which have been available to be observed and are worth remembering.

Perhaps the best way of grasping this truth is the picture which Jesus gives us of salt and light. He said, 'You are the salt of the earth', and 'You are the light of the world'.[2] Salt and light behave in different ways. Salt is subversive. When it is in food people are rarely conscious of it but it does its work of preservation and taste. Light is obvious. We know when it is dark and when it is light: it is not subversive. It was Daniel's ability to be like subversive salt in his second-choice world that opened up the opportunity for him to be as glorious light sometime later.

Second-choice worlds are great environments for doing the work of the gospel. When people see authentic Christian living in times of considerable difficulty and trial the gospel is proclaimed in a way which sermons never could. Sermons are light; second-choice worlds are salt. Second-choice living can be powerfully subversive if we let God do what he wants to do in the middle of it. Once more second-choice worlds become first class in their effect.

Sarah came to live in our house in 1990. She did not know it but she was and still is a subversive. Probably the best subversives are the ones who do not realize they are. Although Sarah is a wonderful friend and a special person she would not stand out in a crowd or be the centre of attention at a large party; she is like the other five million people in London who experience the day-to-day grind of travel, work, social life, sleep and more work. Yet through

---

[2] Matthew 5:13–14.

just living her life, going through her struggles, courageously facing ear operations, expanding her world-view, speaking the truth, facing her fears through learning how to drive and seeking to see what God was doing in the process, she has been a subversive to me. Sarah is not a perfect person, I doubt whether anyone will write a book about her life, ask her to tell her story on the television or invite her to speak at huge Christian congresses but she has made a life-long impact on us. Her great gift has been to take the circumstances she is in, face them squarely and work away at them until they change or she decides to change strategy. She has a wonderful sense of her own reality which is rare and precious. Through living her own life Sarah has become a Daniel. Doing what she needs to do and doing it well in the context of the purposes of God has generated a subversive and powerful life. Many people with much more spectacular gifts than Sarah would benefit from spending time with her, to learn how she does it.

Chapter Twenty-three

Abandon perfectionism

'The bad really is terrible and the good may
seem powerless against that terrible reality,
but when the good and the bad intermingle —
not merge but intermingle — ' . . . They form
a pattern,' said Jon, 'as I pointed out a
moment ago. The darkness doesn't become
less dark, but the pattern which the light
makes upon it contains that meaning which
makes the darkness endurable.'
(Susan Howatch: *Absolute Truths*[1])

What will undo us in our second-choice world are ideas
and aspirations related to perfectionism. These goals are
usually associated with good intentions; they often flourish
in worlds without grace but they tend to be driven by
organizational culture rather than scriptural reality. Daniel
did not live in a perfect world where everything went
smoothly for him. In spite of leading a prayerful and consistent life he was never able to get anywhere near a perfect
world; reality always came crashing through.

---

[1] S. Howatch, p. 637.

Perfectionism has a powerful effect on modern life. The cults of excellence, being slim, fit and seeking to be perceived as a 'winner', all play their part in setting up impossible standards by which people are expected to live their lives. Similar tendencies towards perfectionism sweep around the church, causing individual and corporate confusion wherever they settle. The people who get caught up in them often look like victims of addiction rather than pursuers of perfection.

Christian realism

For many the standards are often set impossibly high. This happens for a series of reasons, some of which have little relation to New Testament reality. To take one example, Amy Carmichael's *If* is devotionally pure and wonderfully aspirational but the standards it sets just seem out of reach.

'If I can enjoy a joke at the expense of another: if I can in any way slight another in conversation, or even in thought, then I know nothing of Calvary love' (p. 8).

'If I belittle those whom I am called to serve, talk of their weak points in contrast perhaps with what I think of as my strong points; if I adopt a superior attitude . . . then I know nothing of Calvary love' (p. 5).

'If I can write an unkind letter, speak an unkind word, think an unkind thought without grief or shame, then I know nothing of Calvary love' (p. 9).

'If I do not feel more for the grieved Saviour than for my worried self when troublesome things occur, then I know nothing of Calvary love' (p. 10).

'If I take offence easily, if I am content to continue in a cool unfriendliness, though friendship be possible, then I know nothing of Calvary love' (p. 36).

'If souls can suffer alongside, and I hardly know it, because the spirit of discernment is not in me, then I know nothing of Calvary love' (p. 47).[2]

The words powerfully convey Carmichael's intensity but they need some explanation in the light of God's love and grace. The whole point of God's love and grace is that when I speak an unkind word or I am not as friendly as I should be he continues to love and show favour to me. Rather than 'falling from grace' when I sin or make stupid decisions I am able to 'fall into grace' through repentance and forgiveness. 'Calvary love' is about people who are in a mess and therefore in a position of need.

If we are to live well in our second-choice worlds we need to understand our relationship with God. Due to the dislocation of the whole cosmos, and the personal dislocation and subsequent deformity of our own lives we live in the middle of sin and evil. Although God gives us a new start through the sending of the Spirit and new birth, not everything is new; we are still ourselves living in our shattered world. We may well have received the benefits of becoming the people of God, we may be walking and talking with him; his grace and love may be ours but these do not transform all of our circumstances and make everything just as it should be. I am sure that some people become Christians anticipating an idealized world which has been presented to them by an enthusiastic evangelist. A few years later, they cannot understand why Jesus does not seem to

---

[2] A. Carmichael, *If.*

be working for them in the way he seemed to work for the evangelist. Added to the inescapable problems of their lives they are carrying a burden of irrelevant and unnecessary guilt.

Jesus and perfection

There is perfection presented in Scripture but it is the perfection of Jesus. The story of his birth, life and death is the unfolding of how absolute love and courage were lived in the mess and chaos of first-century Palestine. The only perfection available to us is his and this comes to us through faith not through a spiritual enterprise, harsh religious regimes or joining a special set of Christians. This does not mean we can then live without caution or escape the desire to be like him. It does mean that we need to be realistic about what can be achieved in terms of personal transformation. If our goals for ourselves are set higher than what can be achieved what does that say about us, our need to exercise control and be seen to be good? If this is a problem, then perhaps we need to go back to the very basis of what the gospel is all about. Simple childlike trust in what Jesus has done through his death and resurrection is the basis of our acceptability before God.

Working together for good?

Many Christians have heard Romans 8:28 quoted, mis-quoted, preached on. The words have been a comfort . . . a joke . . . and a mystery. I have heard many Christians describing the troubles they were going through before ending the conversation with, 'Well, all things work together for good.' They were quoting the King James translation which says, 'We know that all things work together for good to them that love God, to them who are called according to his purposes.'

But do they? Do all things work together for good? Do they really? I don't honestly think they do. The New International Version translation has a different slant: 'We know that in all things God works for the good of those who love him, who have been called according to his purpose.' The idea is not that all things 'work' together for good, but that they intermingle for good. The good does not make the bad good, it stands out in relief against it, making the bad more bearable. It is God who is 'working for the good' but the bad is still around. God is in the middle of the bad, working for our good. The verse does not suggest some flattening out of our human experience into one which can always be called good. Cancer, redundancy, racism and corruption are all bad but good can be at work in the middle of them.

When things don't work out as we planned, the new situation can often shed new light on what was good and bad. The pain of second-choice worlds can give meaning to our lives; it can sometimes demonstrate what is really good and valuable, standing out in contrast to the bad. The pivotal question is whether we will allow God to converse with us in the middle of the contradictions.

We often need our second-choice worlds in the same way as athletes need their exercise machines. They test us for all the challenges which are ahead but they do not make us perfect. We throw ourselves against them so that we can be ready to face our own far from perfect reality. By contrast, experiencing only first-choice worlds will make us flabby, so that when the pressure is on we shall find ourselves unable to accomplish what God intends us to do.

Chapter Twenty-four

Dominant God

It seems to me that we often, almost sulkily,
reject the good that God offers us because, at
that moment, we expected some other good.
(C. S. Lewis: *Letters to Malcolm*[1])

The whole of Daniel's life was a life of response to the initiatives of God. So it mattered very much to him what God was like. Who was this God to whom Daniel responded? It was Daniel's God who handed his people over to Babylon and locked them into prison-like bondage to alien people. Daniel saw God as great, awesome, righteous, merciful, forgiving, faithful, a lover of his people and one who was waiting for a response from them to him. The initiative was God's. The initiative is always God's.

How often we hate this. We tend to like a God who is co-operative with our personal projects of feeling great and looking good. If God has given us a tendency to be overweight or we get less money than we want to, these disappointments or discontents can become the whole focus of our spirituality and the touchstone of whether God is

---

[1] p. 26 (40f.).

interested in us. It is possible that our concerns may be legitimate but when they become dominant this unzips our lives and exposes us to ourselves; our own agenda becomes clear to us and self-loathing is often the result.

In outpatients

A few weeks after my heart attack I found myself entering a new world which I truly wanted to avoid. I usually spend a lot of my time with highly motivated and gifted people — it is one of the privileges of my life — but the world of the sick feels different, at least to me. I was told to go for a blood test so I found myself sitting in a National Health Service waiting room for my name to be called. Kate, a close friend, sat with me as we waited for my cholesterol to be measured. I suddenly realized that I had entered the world of the poor and the old. I asked myself: is this now my world for the rest of my heart-damaged life? In front of me was a woman who looked about twenty-eight. She had four children swirling around her. She looked washed out by life, her children and her present need to keep control in a small and packed waiting room. She was not at all well dressed, her tights were thick and twisted, she was wearing slippers. She looked broke.

I was trying to work out what her life must be like when I noticed a large man along the row. I had noticed his profile earlier but now he lurched to his feet, swayed, and steadied himself. He was about seventy and appeared to be in a world of his own. His skin seemed to be slipping off his face and his mouth just hung open as he shuffled through the waiting room. He knew that a blood sample had to be taken but he could not wait for his name to be called. He insisted that he received attention now. He was on Warfarin, a drug which thins the blood, and one which, as I recall, a friend of mine had speculated would be prescribed for me. I just wanted to get out of that room.

I sat there wondering whether this was going to be my world from now on. How many more waiting rooms like this would there be by the time my problems were sorted out? After years of jetting round the world, speaking in all sorts of locations and being right at the centre of all sorts of wonderful things, this was for me a clear second-choice world.

Not for the first time I realized that I was being sifted and sorted by my second-choice world. I worship the 'God of the Poor',[2] and I focus my life on Jesus, who was surrounded by the poor and the sick. I grew up with poverty. Yet I wanted to get out of that room as soon as I could. Opposite me sat another woman whose face reflected my feelings; every feature expressed rejection of the place and company. I wondered if she worshipped the 'God of the Poor' like me? Was she too struggling with the frame God was placing her in and feeling self-centred in a similar way to me? Could I, can we, let God set the agenda if it leads to this sort of world?

God: focused or self-centred?

My responses to that waiting room were typical of our modern Western individualism and drive. Daniel, by contrast, was living a life of response to the initiatives of God. For Daniel the world was God-dominated and not self-dominated even though aspects of the Babylon experience

---

[2] D. Hughes, p. 1.

must have been repulsive to him. It was God who set up the frame in which Daniel was called to live and Daniel had to take the initiative in this world which had been delivered to him and in no other. This is a very simple idea which emerges from the whole of Christian Scripture. In spite of this it is very difficult for us to grasp. Maybe we are so self-aware and self-centred that it is impossible for us to see beyond our own dreams and self-talk.

Today we are being driven into ourselves in a way which makes us so self-conscious and inward-looking that we find it almost impossible to see a role for any other person in our world, let alone God. The pressures of modern life make it easy not to notice God and the frame he has placed us in. In these circumstances life tends to be 'lived' through a series of addictions and drives: a process of continual kicking to break out of the box we are in. We may not notice our addictions to look good, be accepted by our friends and to be regarded as a success. But from these sources there emerge such modern characteristics as the cult of excellence, the pressure to be first and the pursuit of physical perfection.

To avoid misunderstanding, I need to say clearly that God has not called us to live with the status quo in all areas of our lives; there are many things he calls us to change and many challenges he wishes us to confront. Yet he does desire us to know the things we can and those we cannot change. These may vary during a lifetime. Sometimes what we cannot change in one period of our lives can be changed in another. There are ways in which we are able to discern what to try to change and what to leave alone. Pivotal in this process of decision-making will be our conversation with God, interaction with a mature community, a grasp of Christian Scripture and taking care to mingle it all with faith.

PART FIVE

Jesus and second choice

Chapter Twenty-five

Jesus in heaven and earth

Dark and dull night, fly hence away,
And give honour to this day,
That sees December turned to May.

Why does the chilling winter's morn
Smile, like a field beset with corn?
Or smell like a meadow newly-shorn,

Thus, on the sudden? Come and see
The cause, why things thus fragrant be:
'Tis he is born, whose quickening birth
Gives life and lustre, public mirth,
To heaven, and the under-earth.

We see him come, and know him ours,
Who, with his sunshine and his showers,
Turns all the patient ground to flowers.
(Robert Herrick: from *What Sweeter Music*)

The story of second choice is the story of mission and redemption. Second-choice worlds can be arenas where God
demonstrates his love, grace and deliverance. Jesus shows
us how second-choice worlds can work. Though the way
in which he came to earth, lived his life, died his death and

returned to his Father he indicates the way our lives should be lived.

Was the world of Jesus a world of second choice? Not in the sense in which our second-choice worlds are for us. His purpose was to work out the way of redemption for us through becoming God in the flesh. Jesus did not become man by accident or tumble into a world which was not his choice. He was able to leave heaven, come to earth, live his life, become a curse, die a criminal death and rise from the dead — and do it all deliberately. He lived through a second-choice world which was his first-choice intention.

Jesus reached out to us because of his love, a love so consistent, passionate and clear that he was prepared to follow its implications and pursue us whatever the cost. It meant his beard was torn from his face, he was spat upon by soldiers, the nails were driven into his body on a cross, he was separated from his Father, became a curse and was slaughtered like a helpless lamb.

Jesus is the redeemer who integrates heaven and earth and in doing so shows us how we can live in a similar fashion. Jesus did not live in a schizophrenic split world. He was not 'heavenly' at one moment and 'earthly' the next. He took on flesh and the material world, becoming a baby. Although we think of God as almighty and all-knowing, Jesus became 'all-powerless, all-vulnerable God who completely depends on us'.[1]

Jesus embraced the chaos and dislocation of our self-sick world and made sense out of it. He did not stand at a distance and wait for everything to be prepared for him so that his life would be problem-free. The whole meaning of the gospel is that Jesus came to bring about transformation. His life was about giving a dislocated world the chance to

---

[1] H. Nouwen, *Bread for the Journey*, p. 75.

come into alignment with God and itself. Jesus headed for trouble with the consistency and insistence of an arrow from a bow. He penetrated the darkness with the exploding light of his focused presence and night-time was turned to day.

Jesus lived in consistent relationship with his Father. The gospels show that Jesus did not take on anything alone. He was in constant communion and collaboration with his Father and the Holy Spirit. The three-in-one and one-in-three God works in diversity and unity to bring transformation out of our lostness and confusion. Yet Jesus went through the process of learning obedience. The writer of Hebrews actually says that he 'learned obedience'.[2] He was not mentored in the sense in which we need to be mentored, but he did grow in 'wisdom and stature'[3] while he was obedient to God and his parents.

Jesus lived subversively. He came obscurely in the womb of a Palestinian woman with little influence or status. He waited until the age of thirty before he started the public phase of his life. Even when he was preaching and healing the sick he was often elusive. Many times he did not give a direct answer to questions, and even answered questions with questions. He told stories the meaning of which people had to work out for themselves. He did not come crashing and crushing, he came both with openness and stealth. He brought a tiny mustard seed kingdom, which in the end will dominate the whole earth, toppling political, economic and military kingdoms, and through this bring peace.

Jesus does not demand that we live with 'perfectionism'. Although he is himself perfect he reaches out to us in the middle of our imperfect lives and makes them work. He

---

[2] Hebrews 5:8.
[3] Luke 2:52.

does desire us to be holy, yet he can work with us when we are not. He is able to do this because he is the one who has already dealt with our imperfections on the cross. His grace reaches out to us, picks us up, speaks words of encouragement which strengthen us and sends us on our way.

Jesus submitted himself to the burden given to him by his Father. Even on the cross when he wanted relief from the agony of death he was determined to live in response to his Father's will. Even though he had all the power to release himself he rejected that option. Rather, he pointed himself in the direction of humankind, submitted to his task and headed for curse and death.

Jesus lived redemptively. He entered into our dislocation to heal our twisted and broken lives. Is it possible to see similar redemption demonstrated in our worlds of second choice? Can we deal with our second-choice worlds in the way in which Jesus dealt with his earthly experience? Can we see our pain, disappointments and difficulties as opportunities for us to really live our lives to the full and see them work redemption in our world? The gospel says we can. We may not be able to do everything well, we may not be brilliant in any sense, but we can see the places where we have to live transformed into places where we want to live because God meets us there with his grace and love.

Jesus is able to bring about transformation in our personal circumstances. But the possibilities are both wider and more profound than that. Through him we can engage, embrace and maybe even observe the transformation of the world around us. Daniel did this. Our second-choice worlds can become arenas of mission, the places where God displays his power, grace and love to a world in need. This was how Daniel lived his life. With his dislocation and vulnerability Daniel faced the Babylonian world and saw God do his work of transformation. A similar work can be done today through us in our churches, communities and jobs. It is Jesus as ever who strengthens us and shows us the way. He calls us to live lives larger than our immediate circumstances. Well aware of our inadequacies, stupidities, vulnerabilities and sins, he points us towards a dislocated world and through the empowering of the Spirit says: 'Go.'

Author's Note

It is over a year since I had my Hyderabad heart attack and I am now back to full and robust health. Due to the speed and skill of my friends and doctor I have sustained very little heart damage. I am now fitter than I have been since I was in my late twenties. I have lost some weight and eat all the right things, am exercising enthusiastically three times a week and have an excellent cholesterol level. I have recently — one year after the heart attack — returned from another visit to Hyderabad. I visited the hospital and various locations associated with the trauma. We all had a great time. What have I learned from that particular second-choice experience? I can feel another book working away inside to help me answer that question.

Future Leader

VIV THOMAS

ISBN 0–85364–949–9

Leadership is a key to success in any organisation.

All the more reason to get it right, says Viv Thomas in a book that sets out to discern the kind of leadership that is needed as we enter a new millennium.

Drawing on biblical models and organisational management research, along with personal experience of some of the evangelical world's most influential leaders, the author provides a model of leadership that is:

- Driven by compassion, not obsession.
- Rooted in relationships, not systems.
- Promotes life, not self-image.

If we fail in these areas, he argues, most of what we do in terms of goals, strategies, skills, mission and communication will eventually be blown away.

This stimulating and inspiring book will test all who might aspire to lead.

VIV THOMAS is the International Co-ordinator of Leadership Development with Operation Mobilisation. He has a world-wide preaching and teaching ministry, with an emphasis on developing leaders. He is also a visiting lecturer at All Nations Christian College in Hertfordshire.

paternoster
press

Cultural Change and Biblical Faith

JOHN DRANE

ISBN 0–85364–979–0

Western culture is undergoing a massive paradigm shift in the course of which our entire style of being will be radically transformed. The changes now taking place are already highlighting areas of discontinuity and contradiction that are impacting life not only in the West, but all over the world.

In this fascinating examination of the future of the church in light of cultural change, John Drane takes as diverse issues as the death of Princess Diana, Environmentalism, film, and the New Age Movement to present ways in which the church should respond in order to be an effective and culturally relevant witness.

JOHN DRANE teaches Practical Theology in the Department of Divinity at the University of Aberdeen, Scotland. He is also an adjunct professor in the School of Theology at Fuller Seminary, California.

paternoster
press

Crying in the Wilderness

DAVID SMITH

ISBN 0–85364–811–5

In this authoritative study, David Smith weeps over a culture now all but lost to the Gospel that shaped it and suggests the approach that Christian witness might take in the twenty-first century. This new contribution to the debate about secularisation is marked by the pronounced pastoral compassion that informs the author's scholarship.

David Smith captures the cries of anguish that can be heard coming from the culture – from secular novelists, painters and philosophers for whom 'God is dead' – as well as the despair experienced from far beyond the confines of 'high culture'.

REV DR DAVID SMITH is Co-Director of the Whitefield Institute in Oxford and a Fellow of the College of Preachers. Formerly Principal of Northumbria Bible College, he is also author of *Transforming the World? – The Social Impact of British Evangelicalism* (Paternoster Press, 1998).

paternoster
press

The Nature of Hell

A report by the Evangelical Alliance Commission on Unity and Truth Among Evangelicals (ACUTE)

ISBN 0–95329–922–8

These days, popular notions of hell tend either to consign it to the realms of fantasy, or to reserve it for the very worst of villains. The biblical picture is quite different, but even very conservative Christians disagree on certain aspects of that picture.

Evangelicals have traditionally held that unbelievers will be condemned without exception to eternal conscious punishment. However, increasing numbers of evangelical thinkers are declaring sympathy for 'conditional immortality'.

These issues are tackled in this report by a special Working Group of the Alliance Commission on Unity and Truth among Evangelicals (ACUTE). The report aims to be biblical and pastoral, and to be accessible to interested lay people as well as to theological specialists.

acute